Coloring Book for Adults

100 Relaxing Mandalas

Stress Relieving Mandala Design for Adults Relaxation

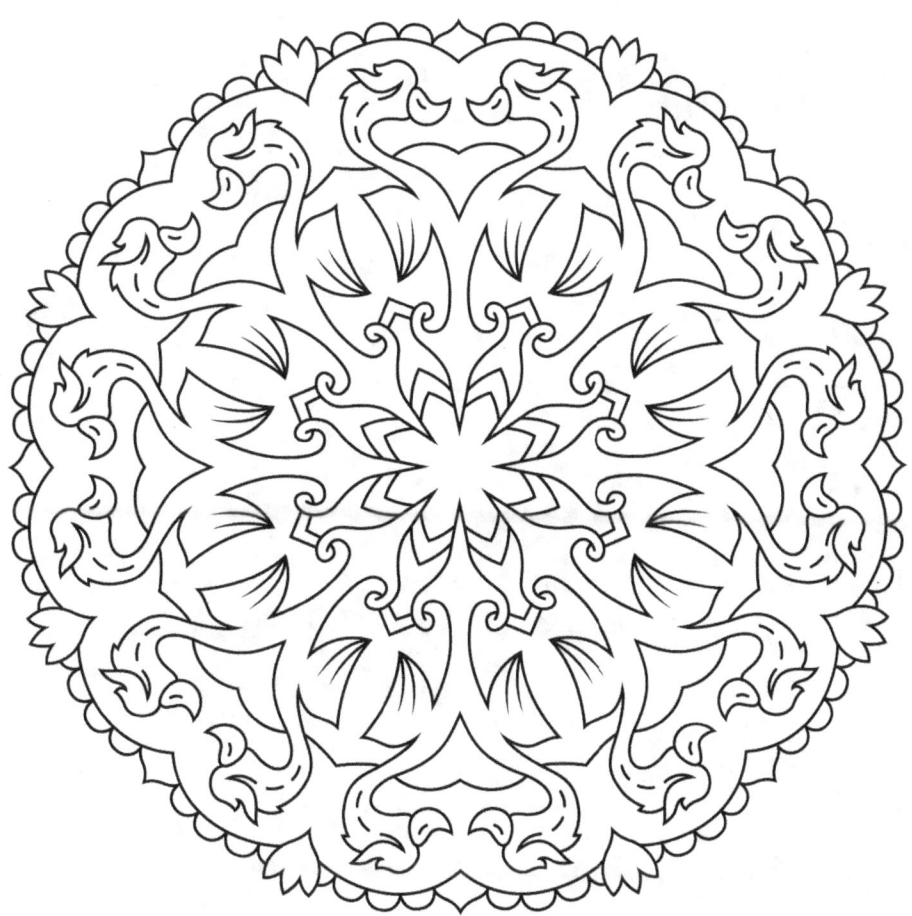

This Coloring Book belongs to :

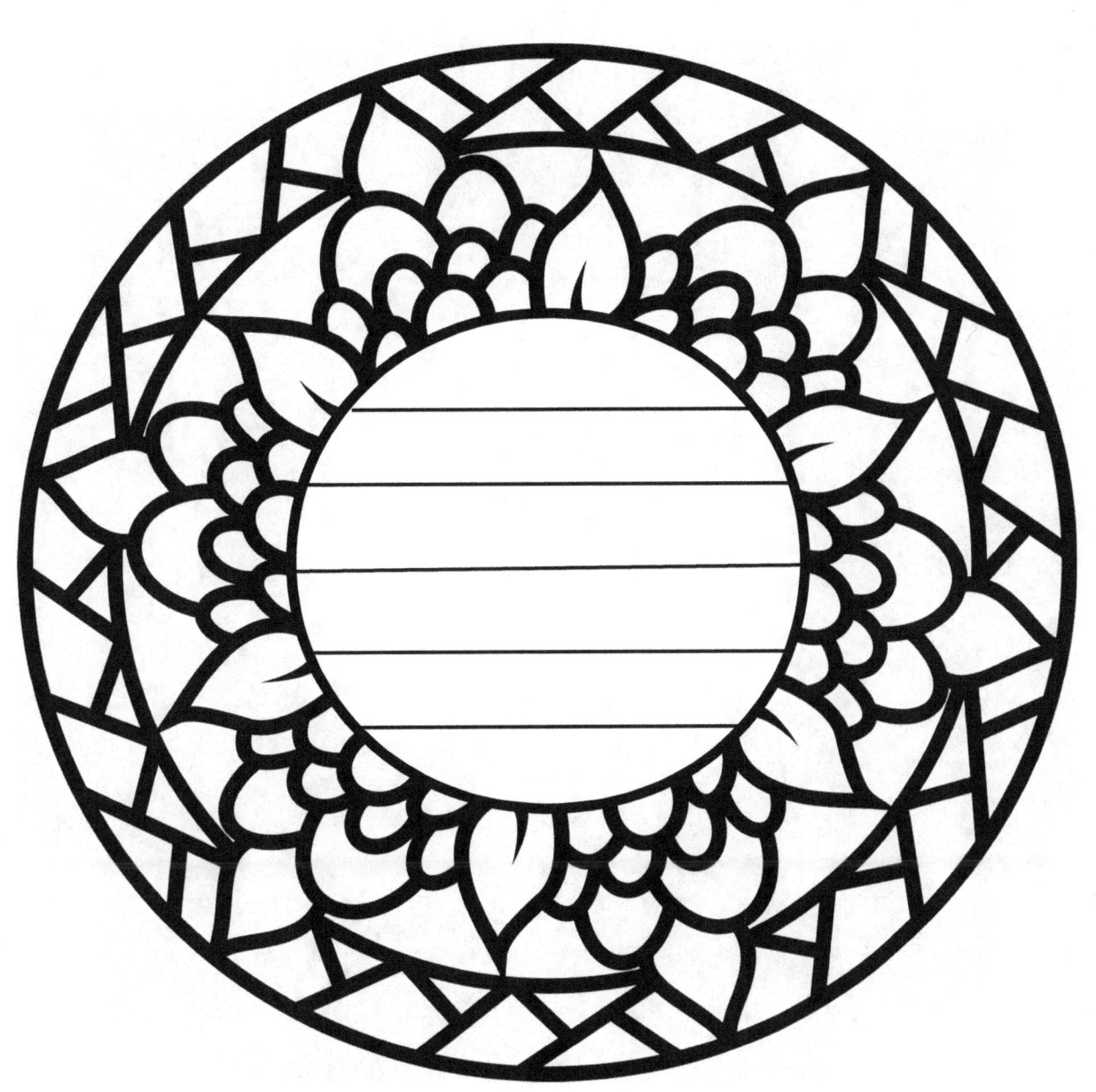

Color Testing

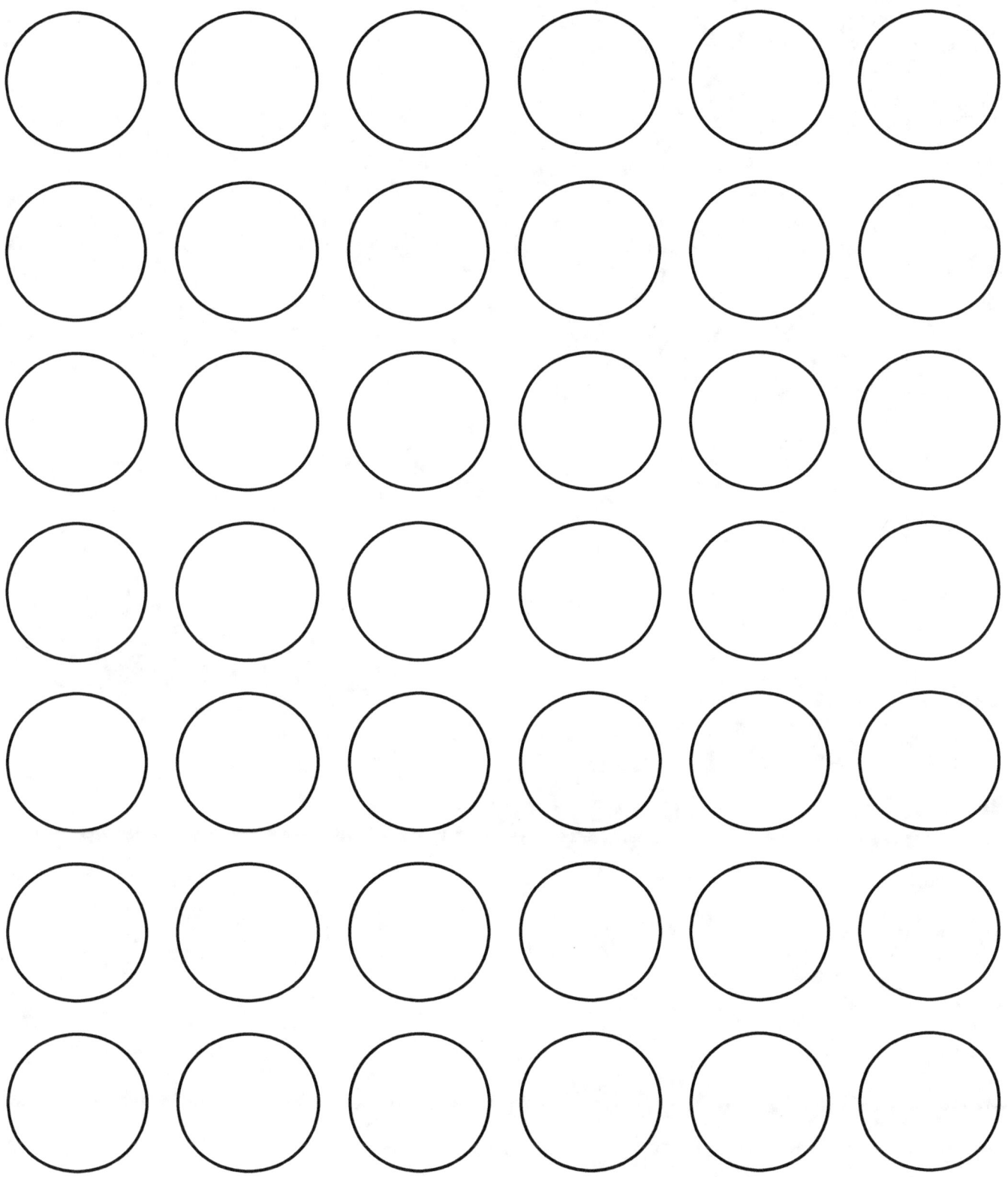

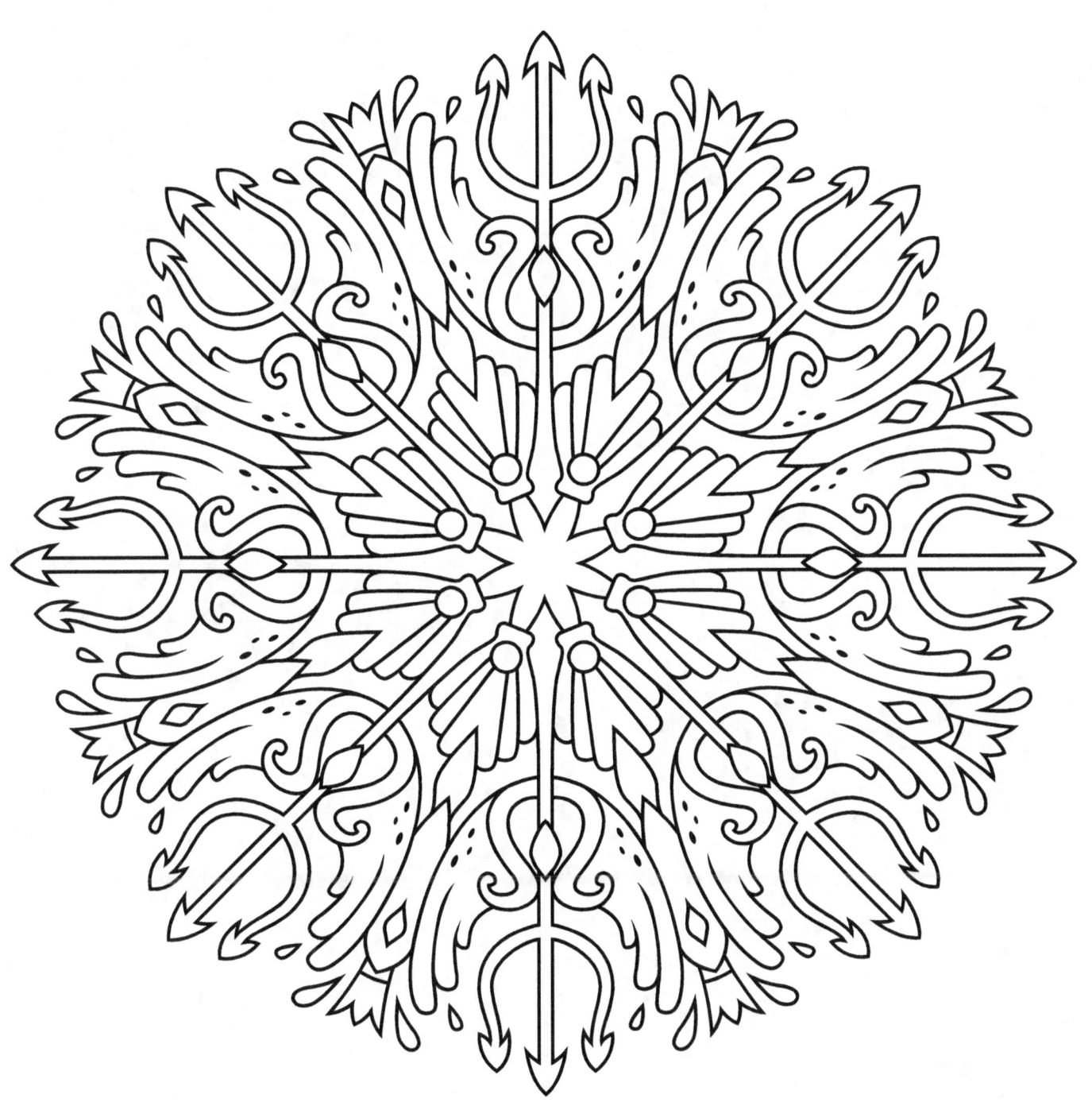

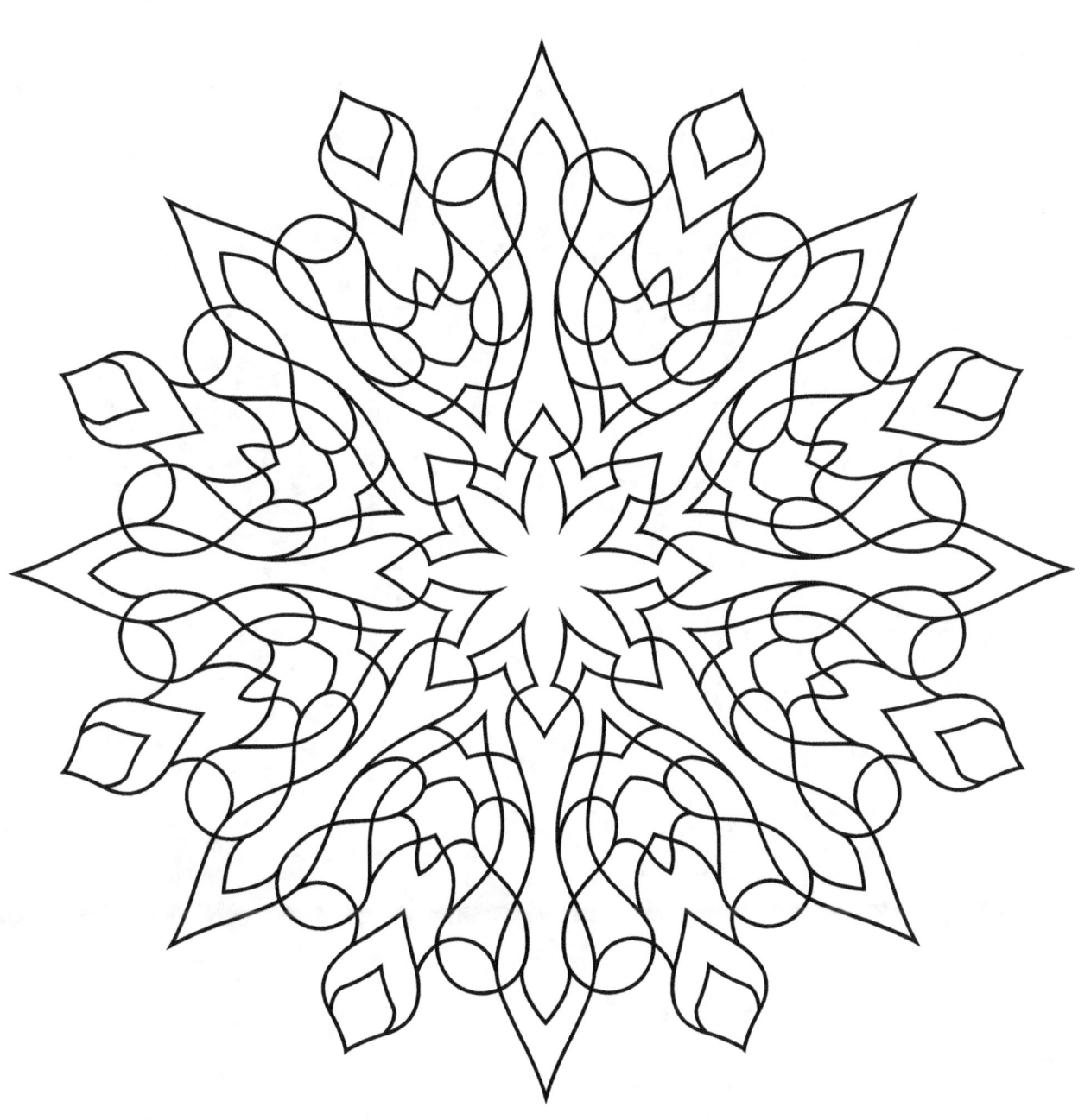

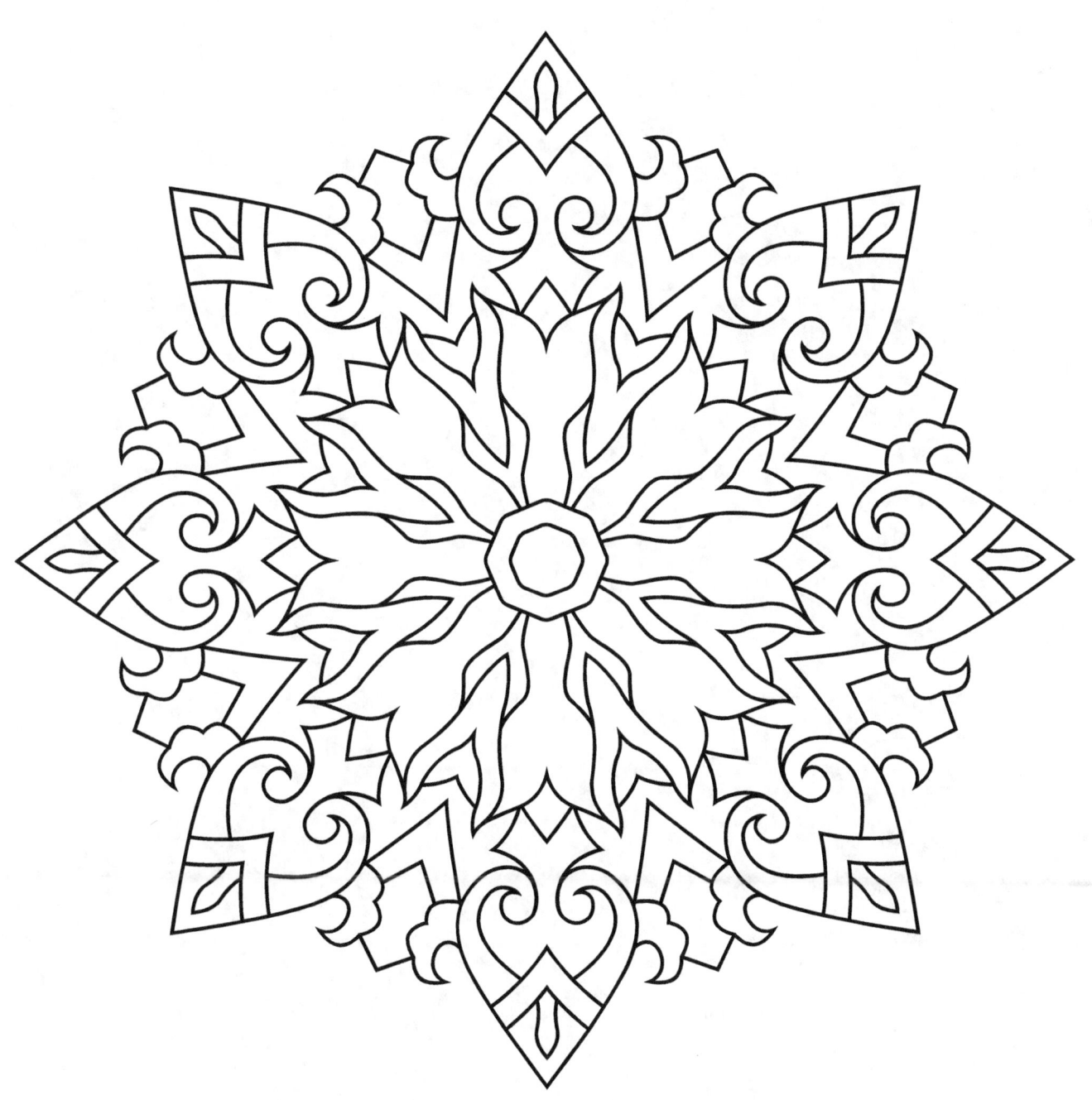

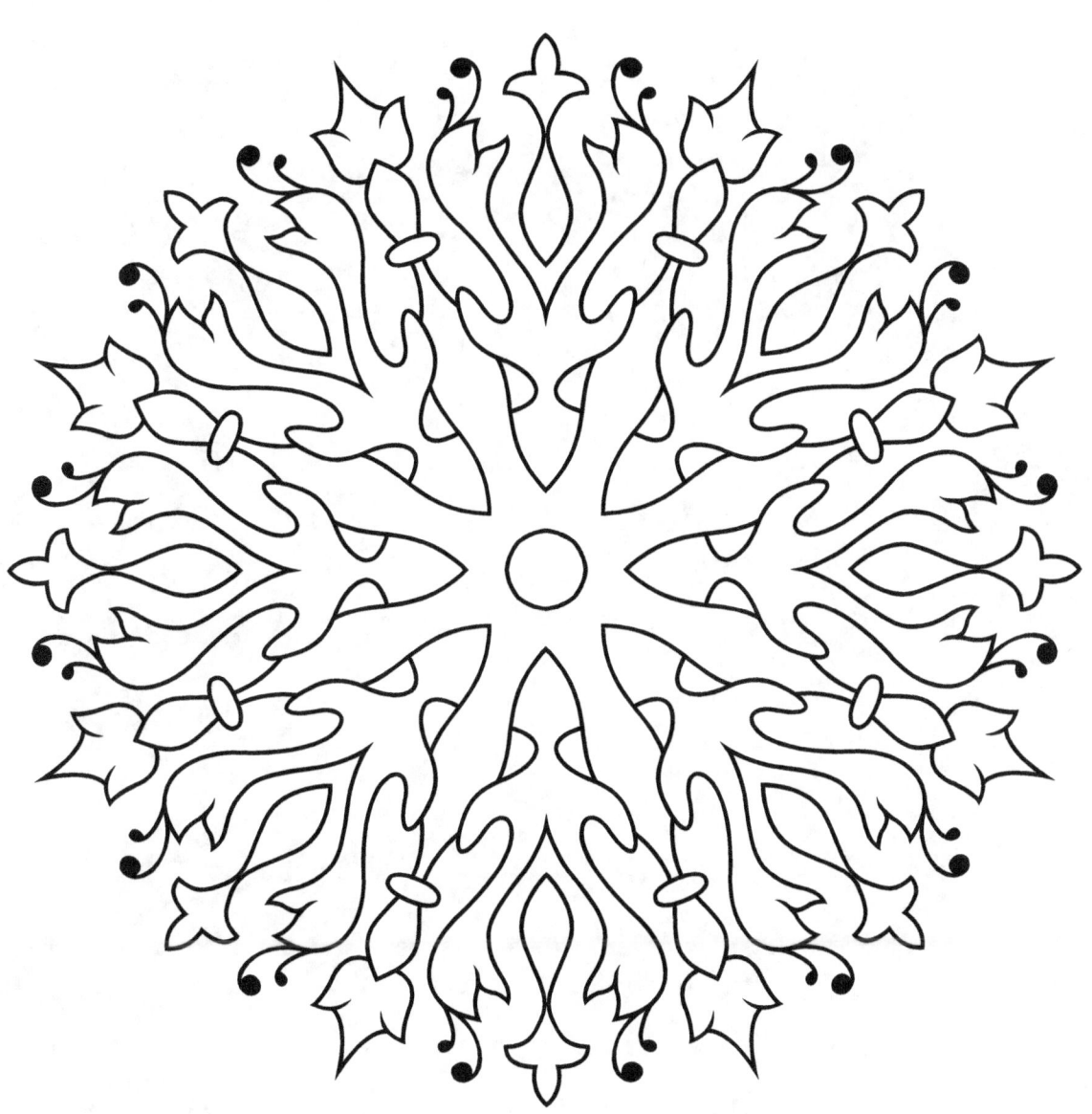

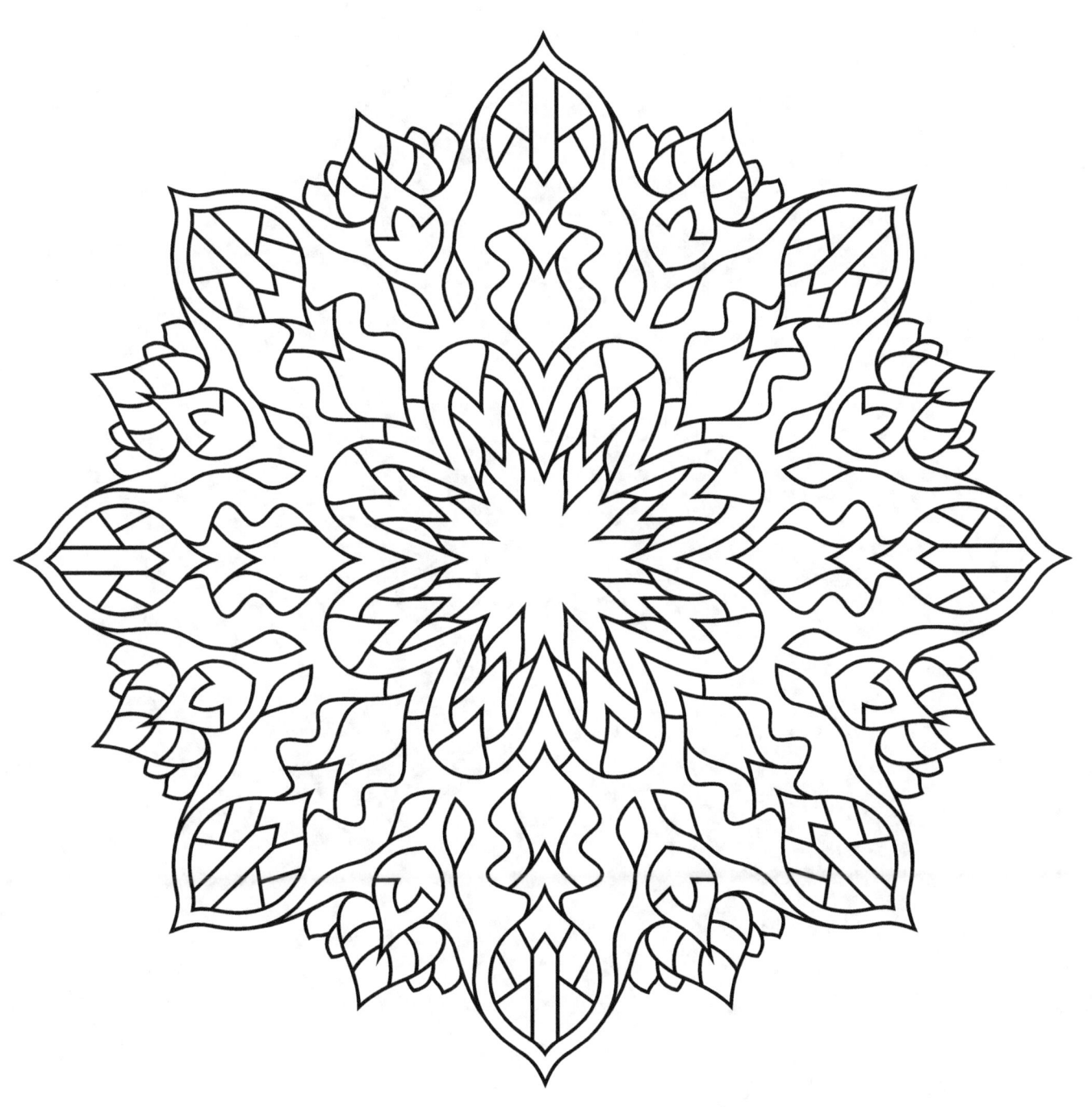

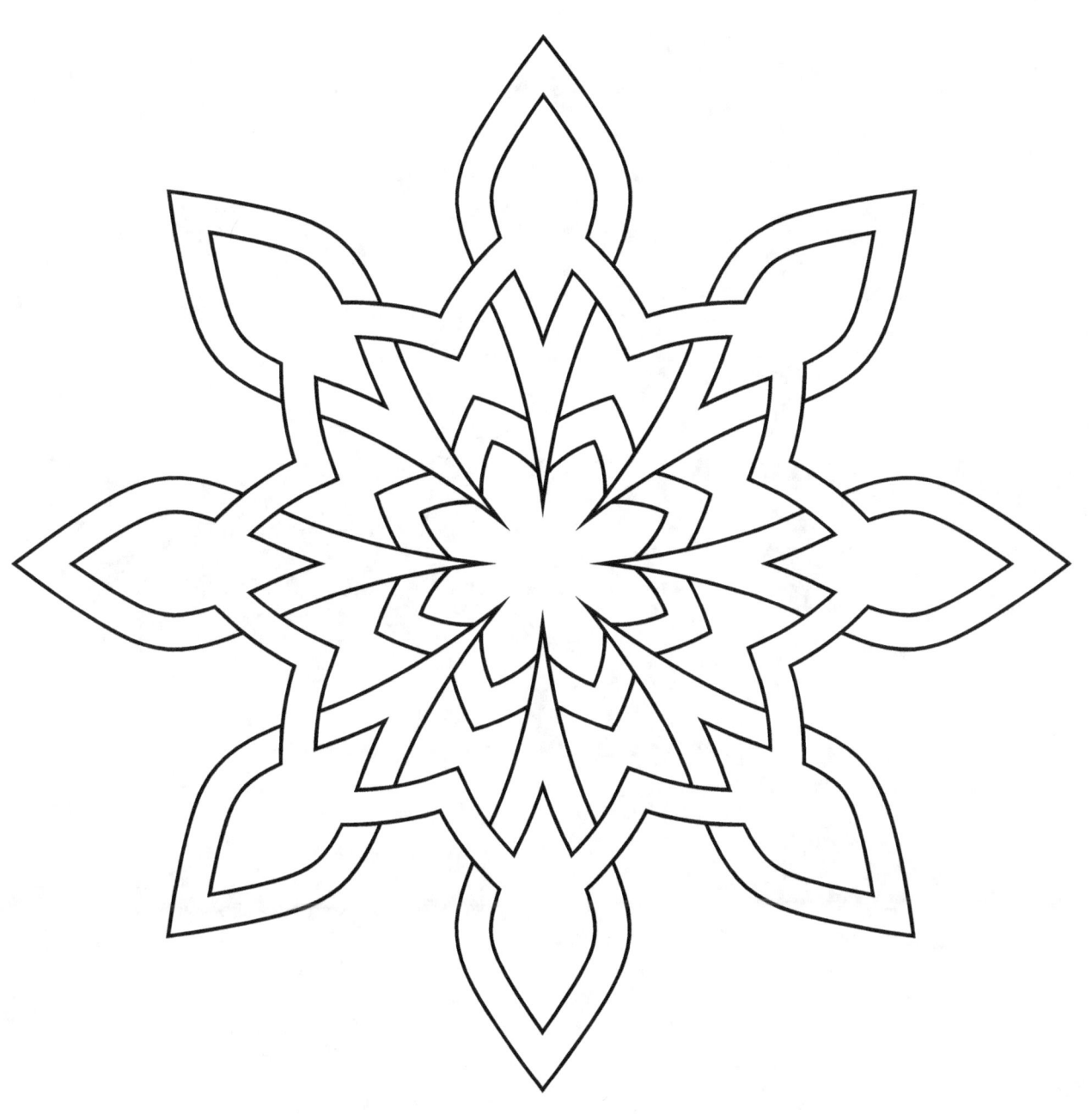

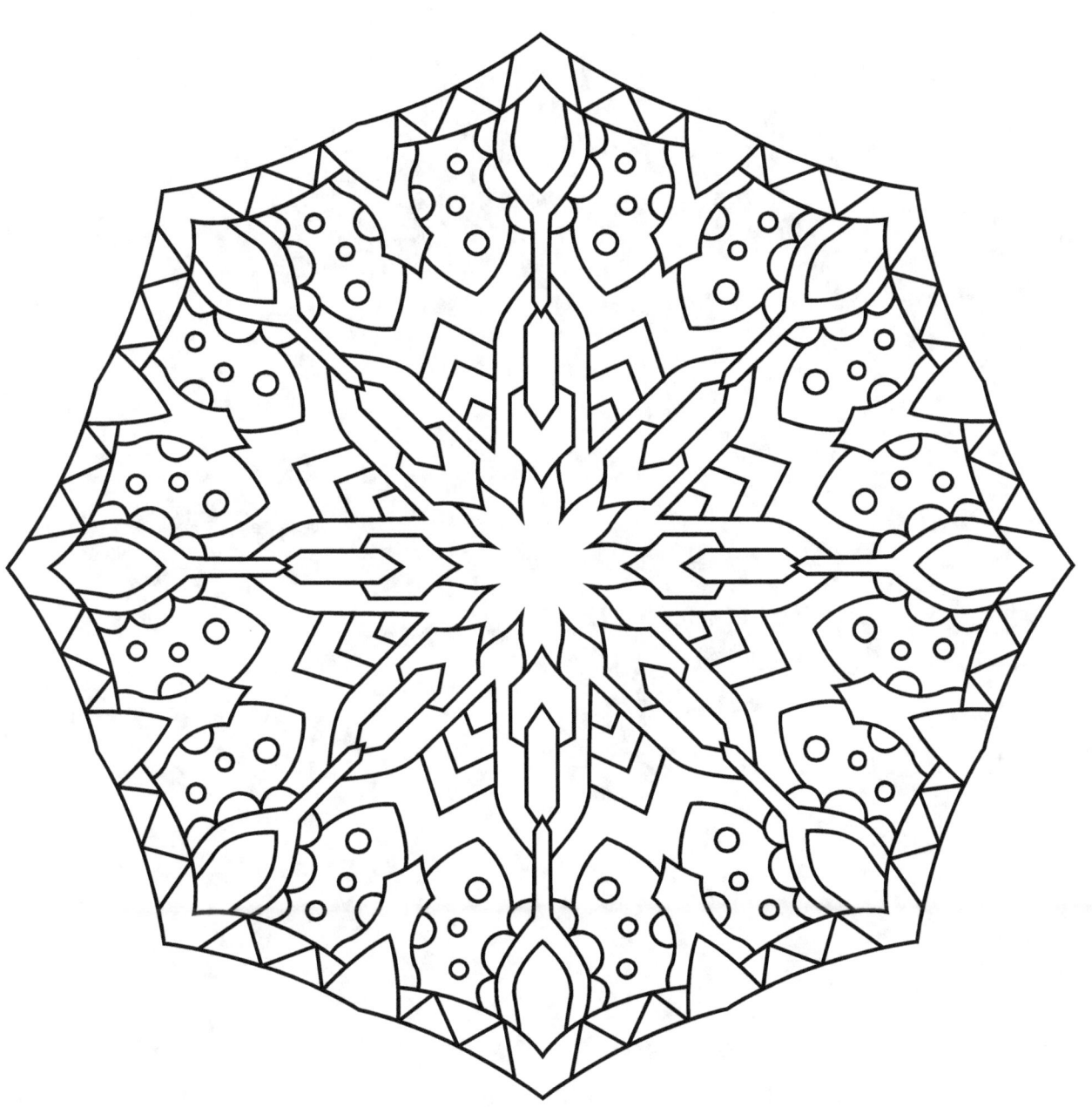

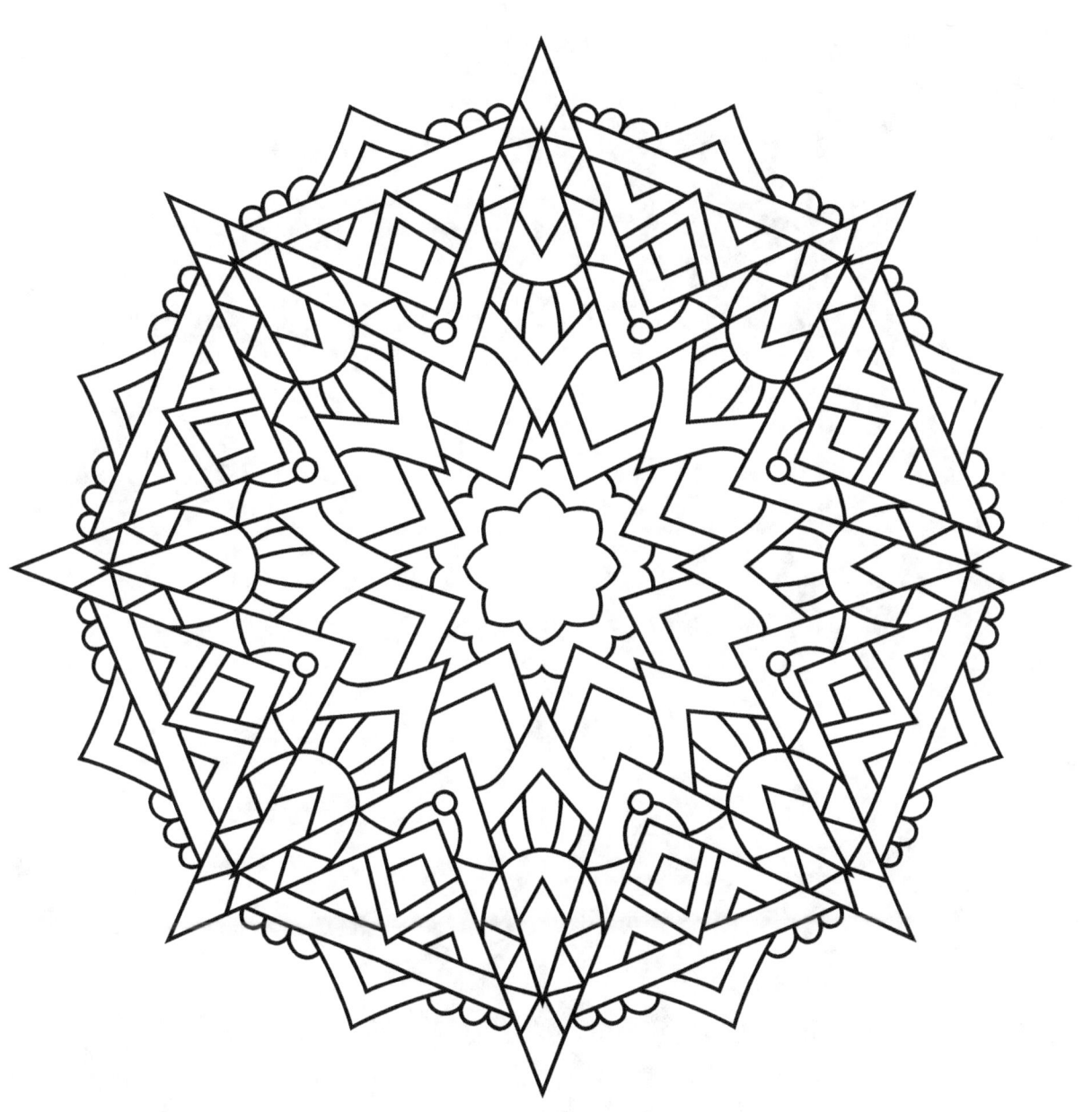

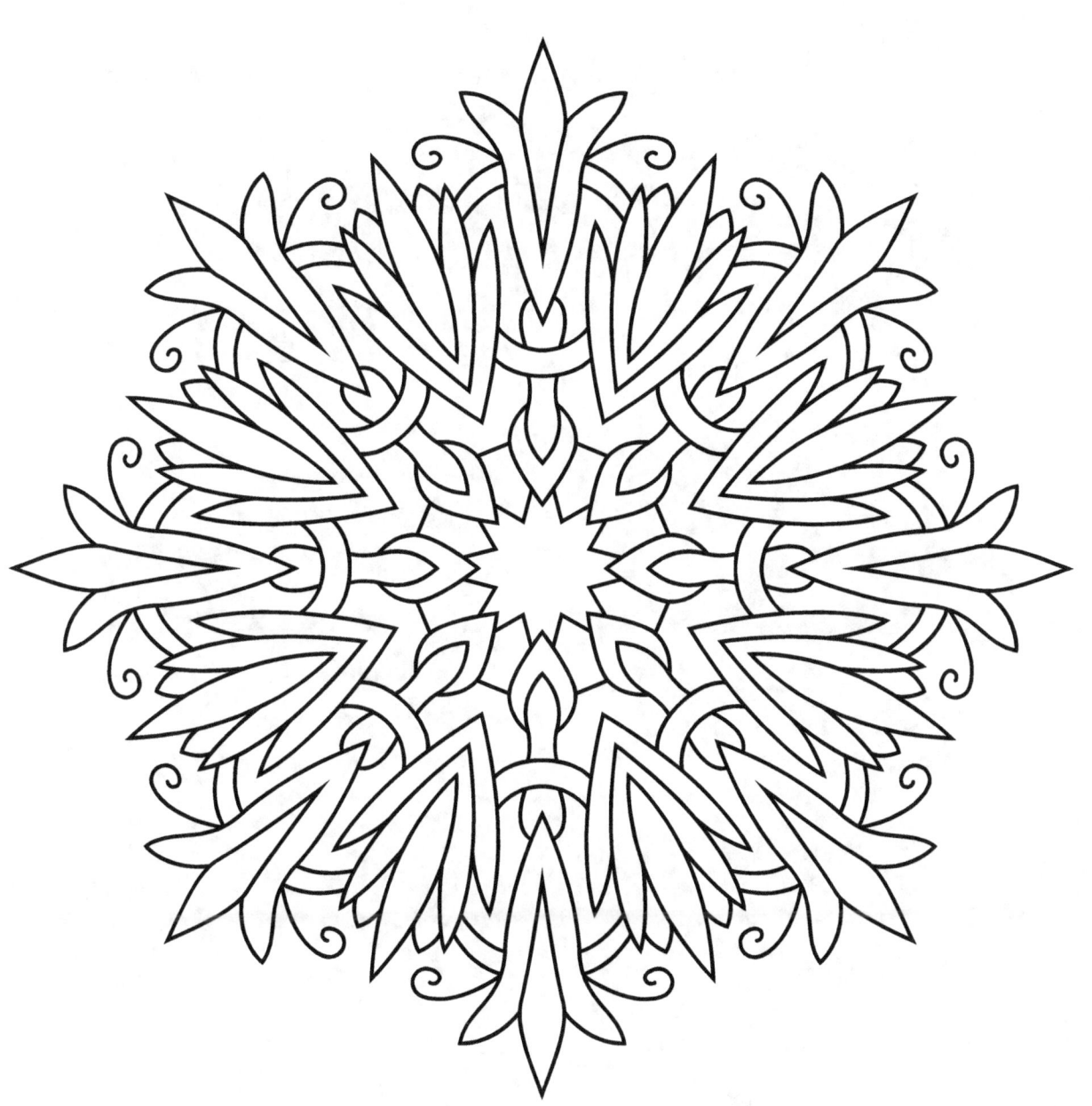

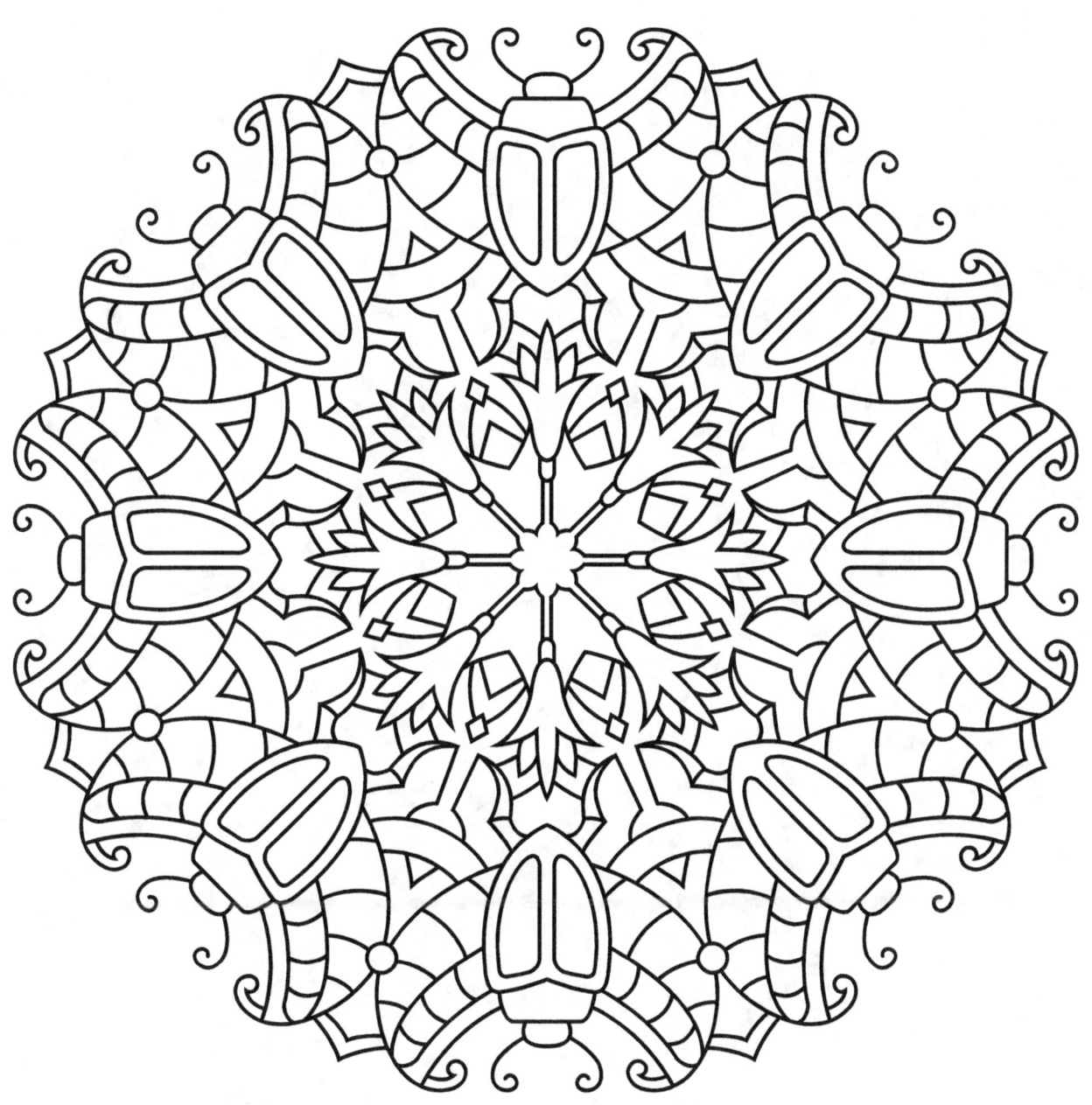

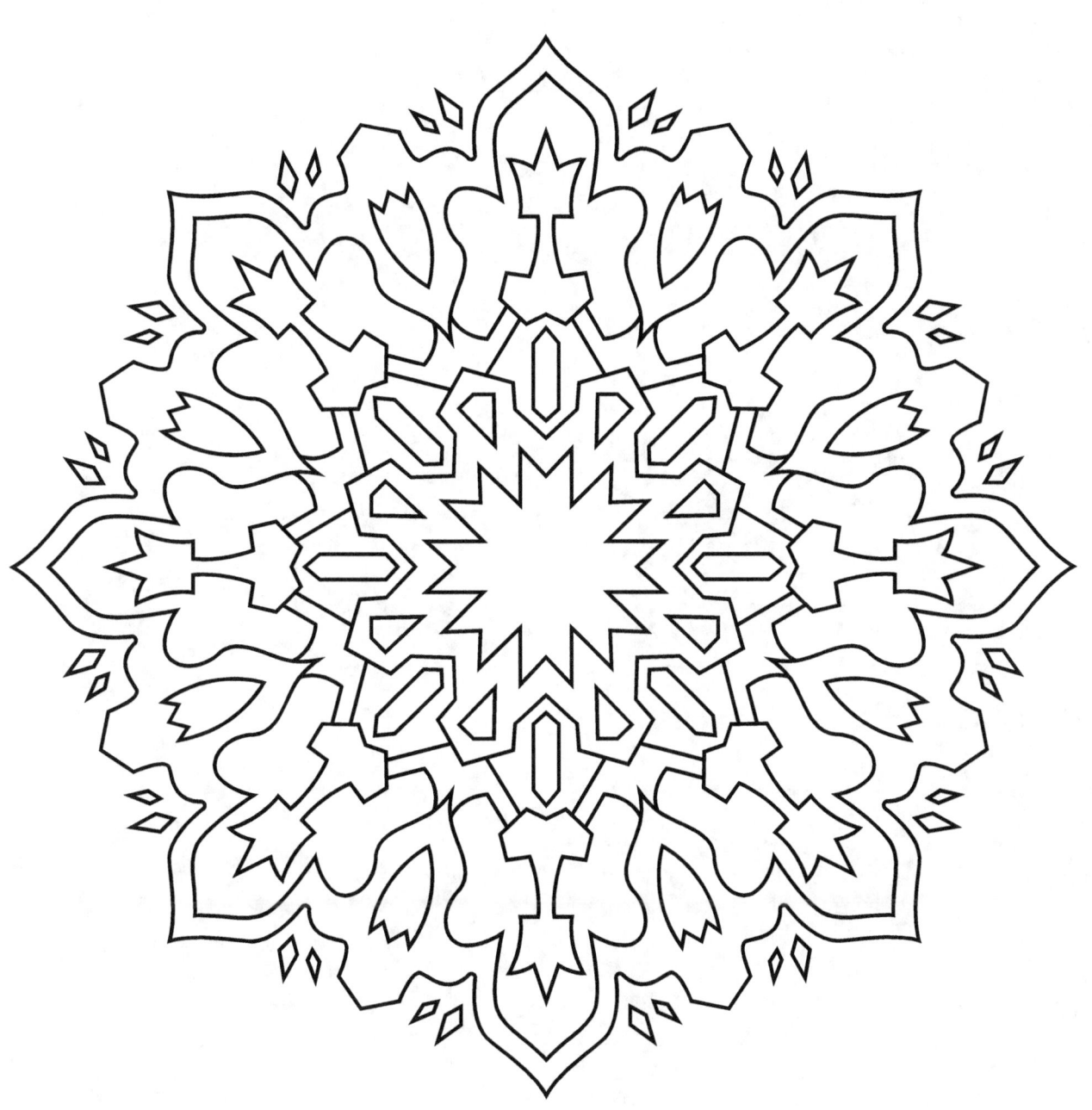

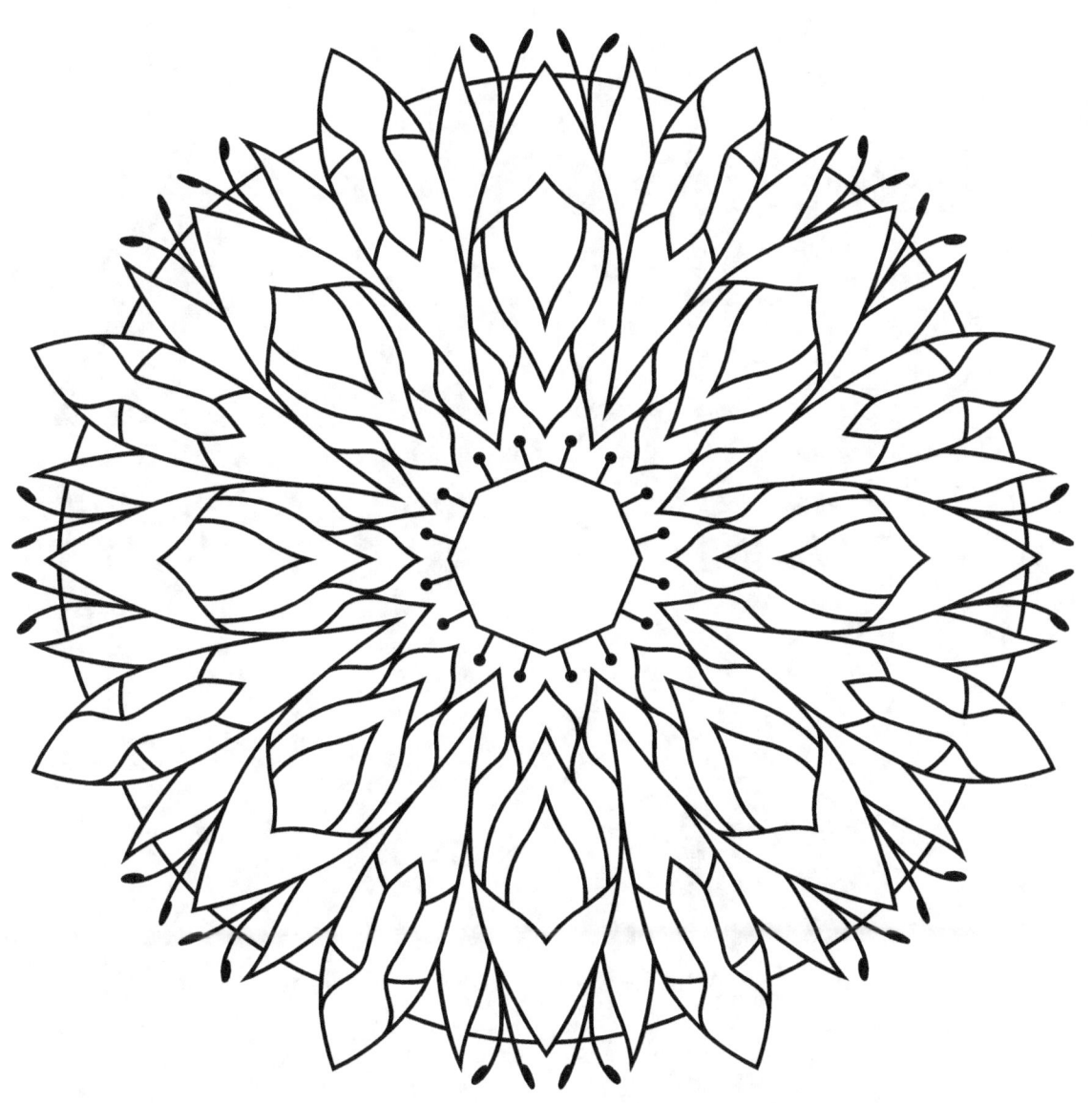

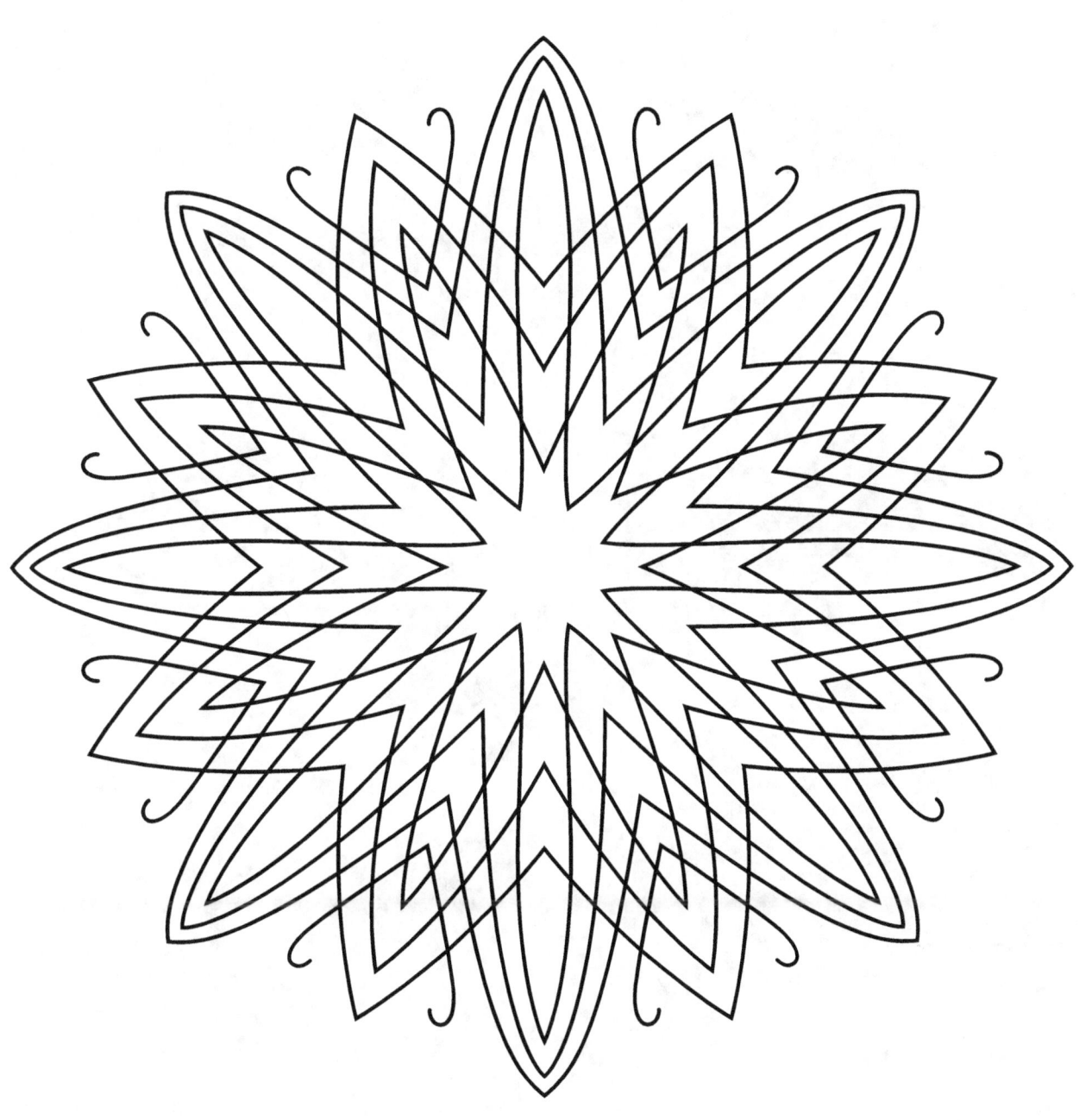

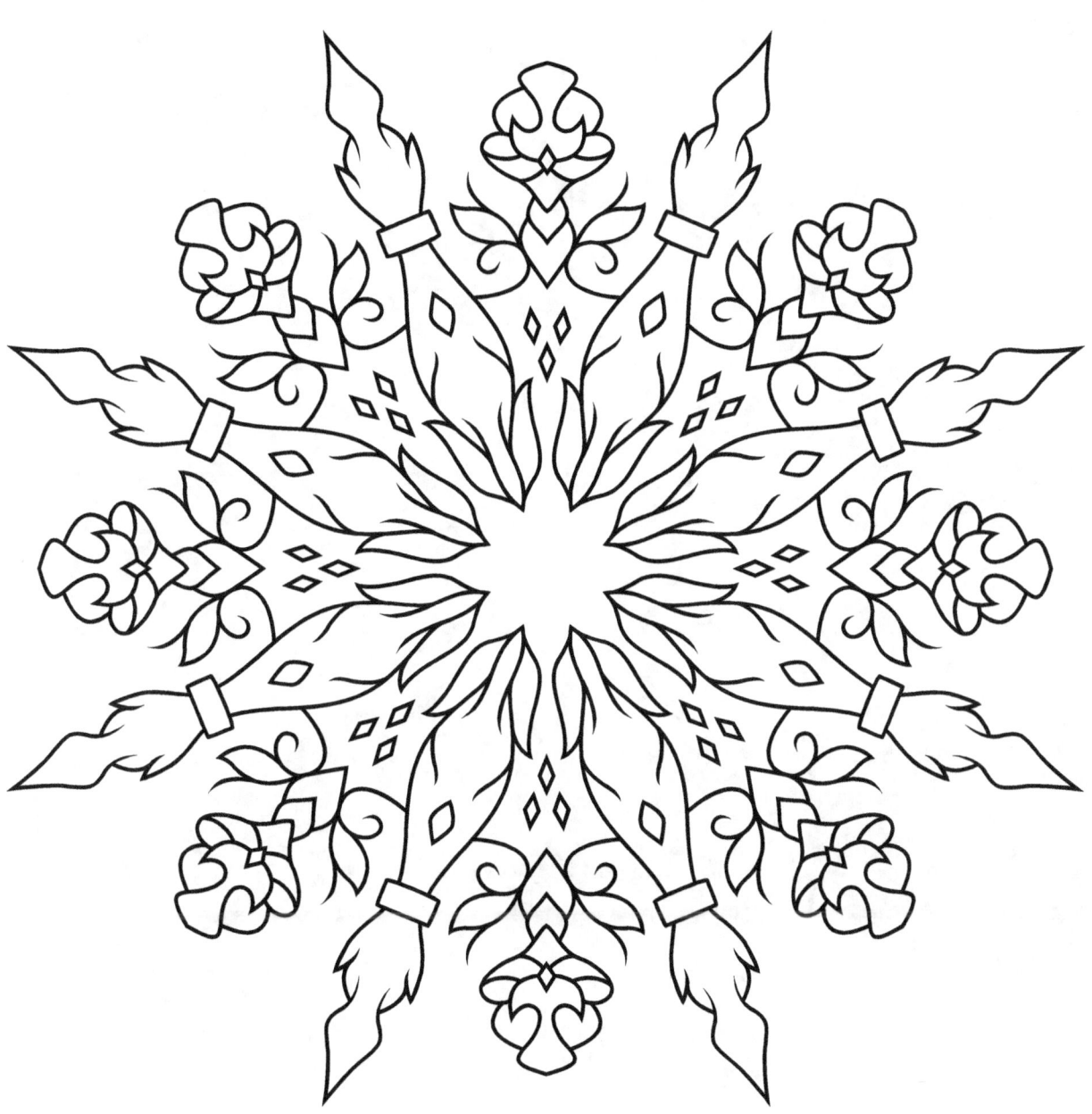

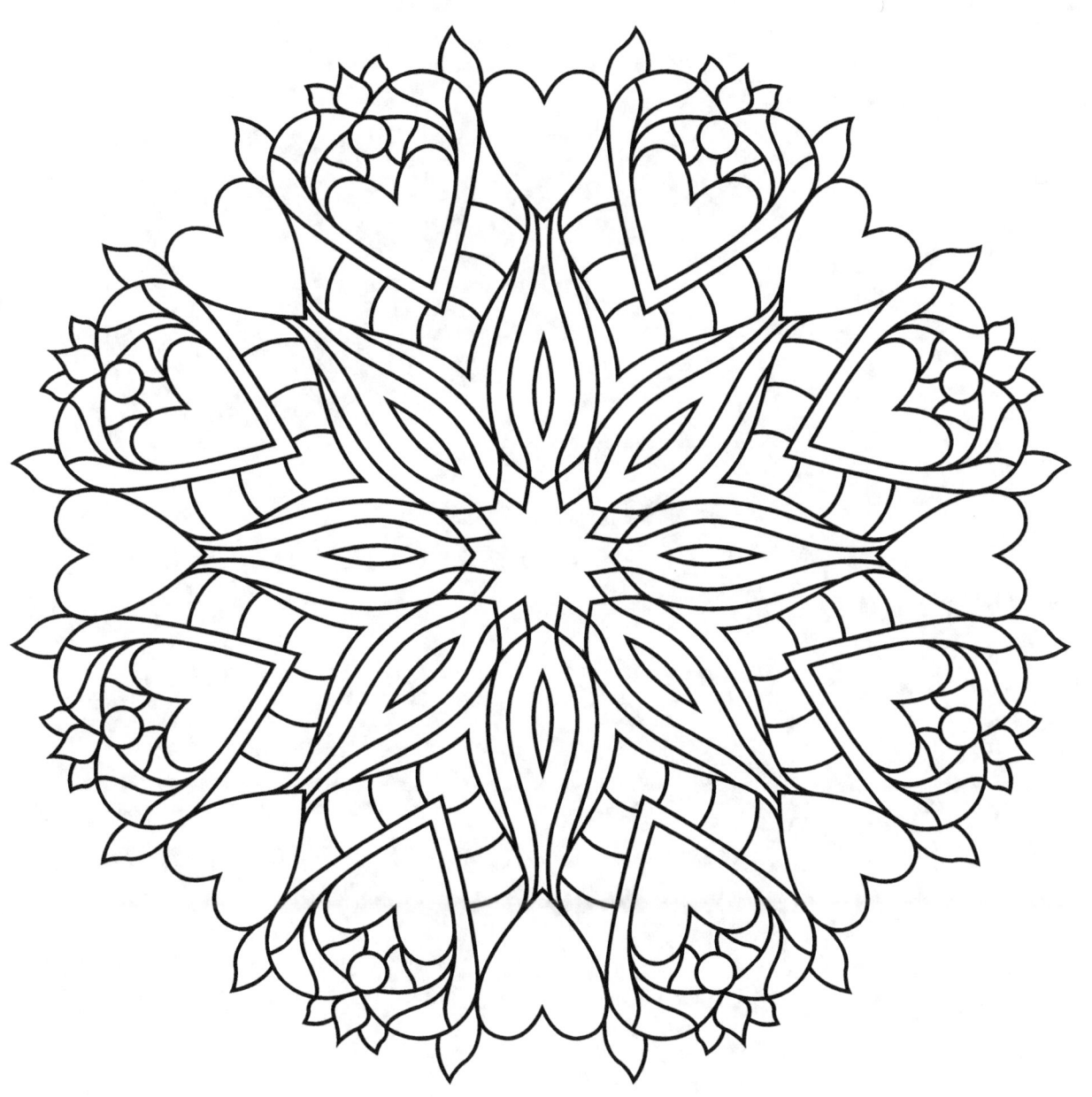

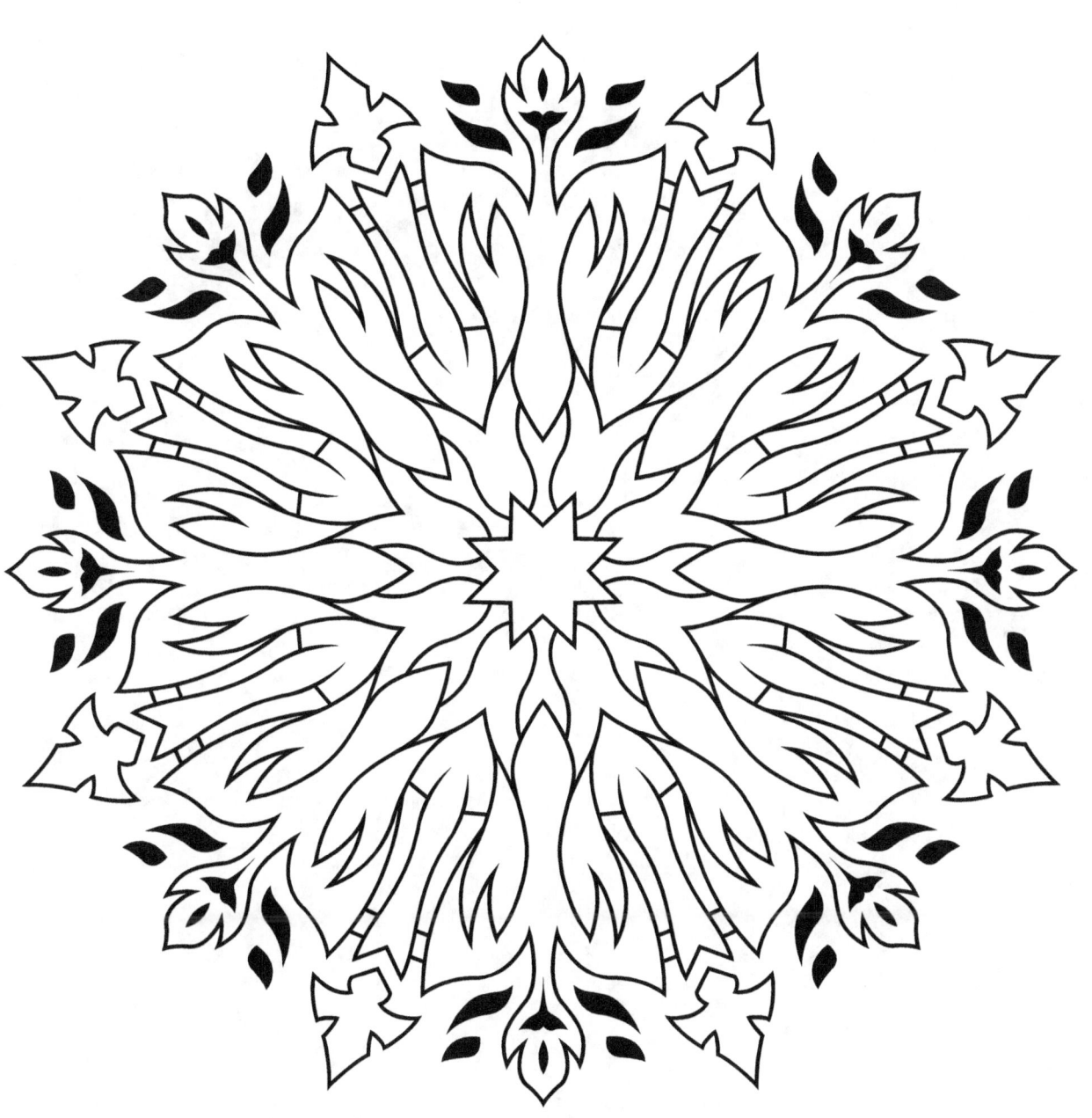

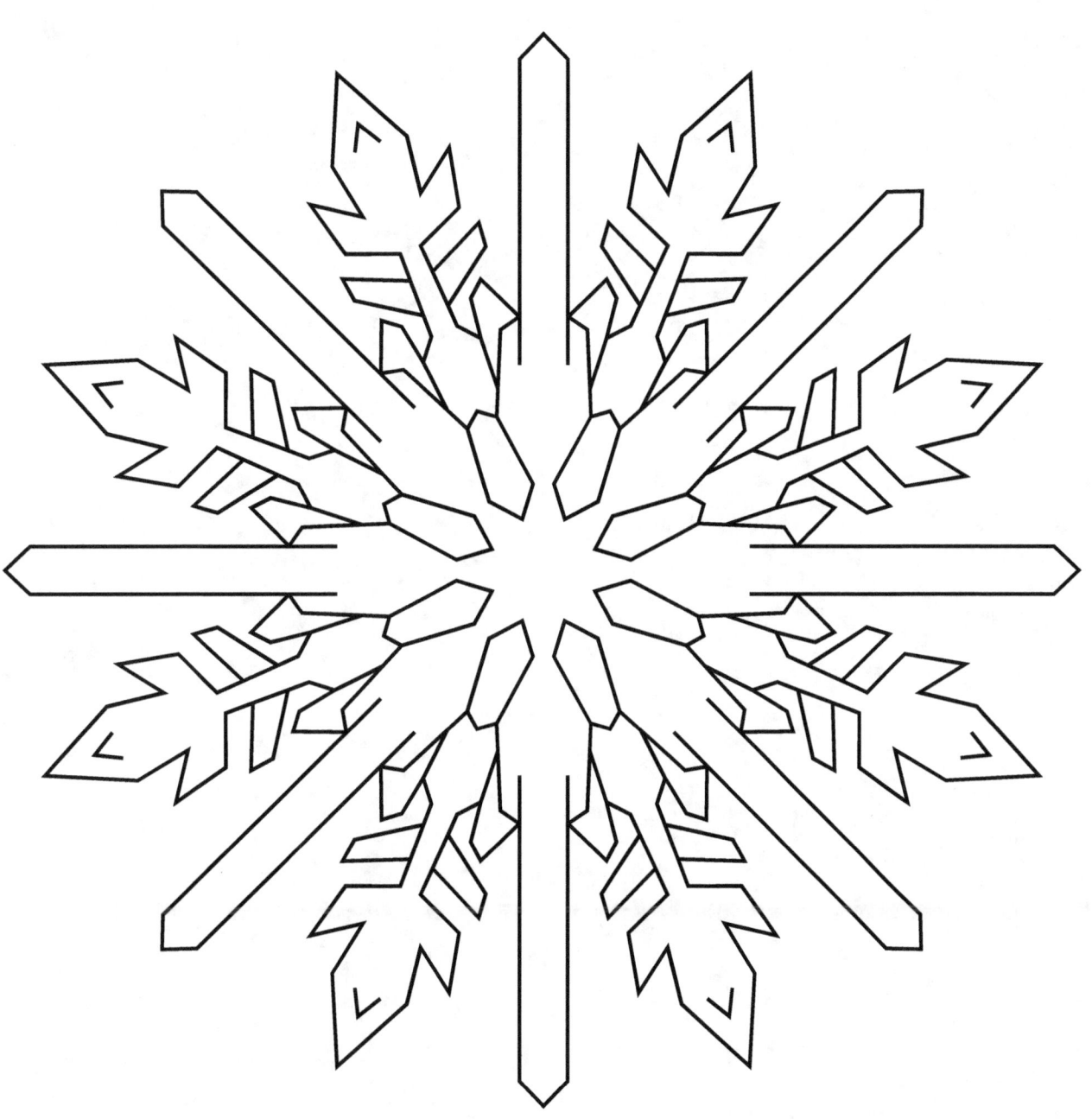

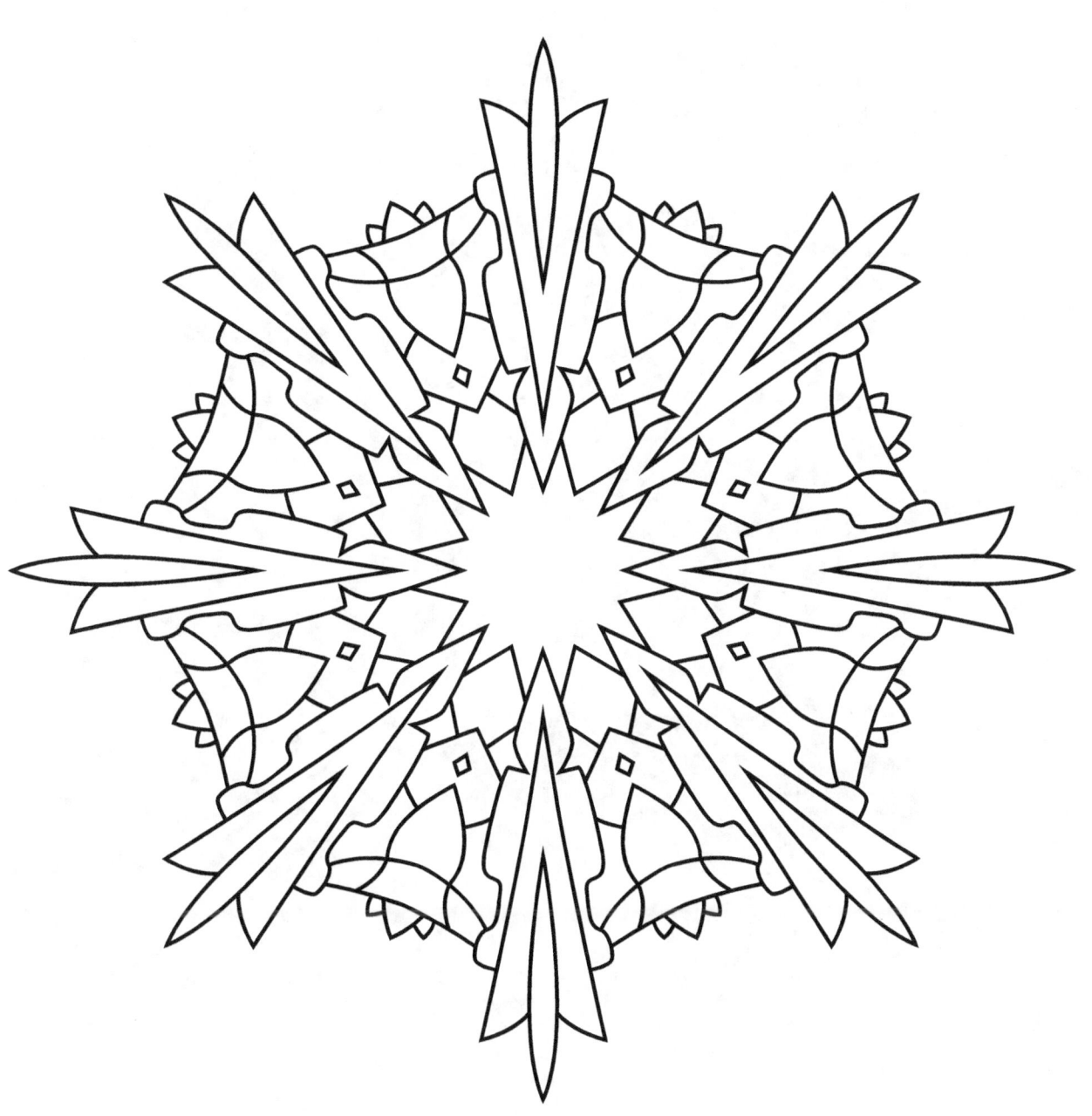

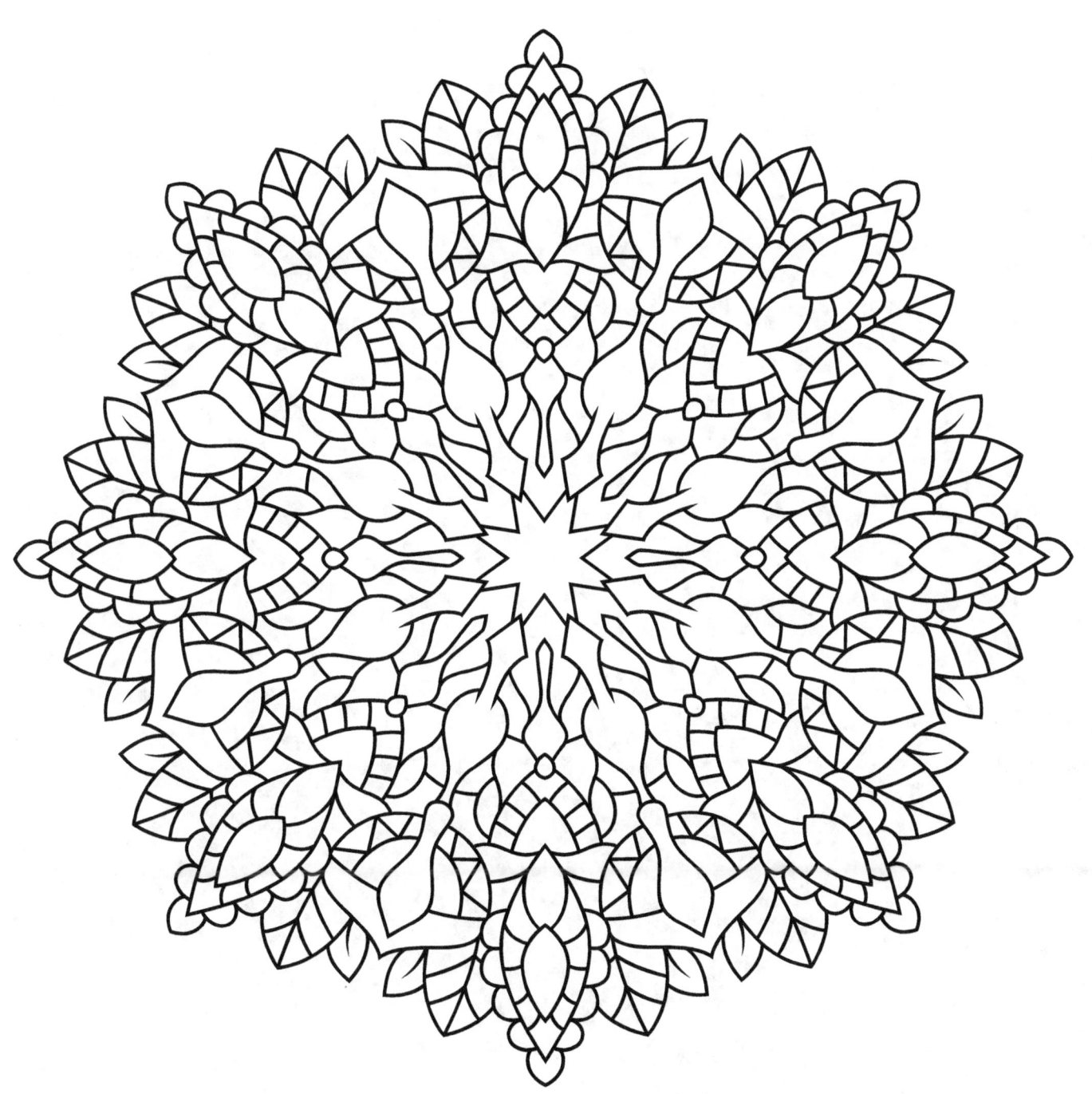

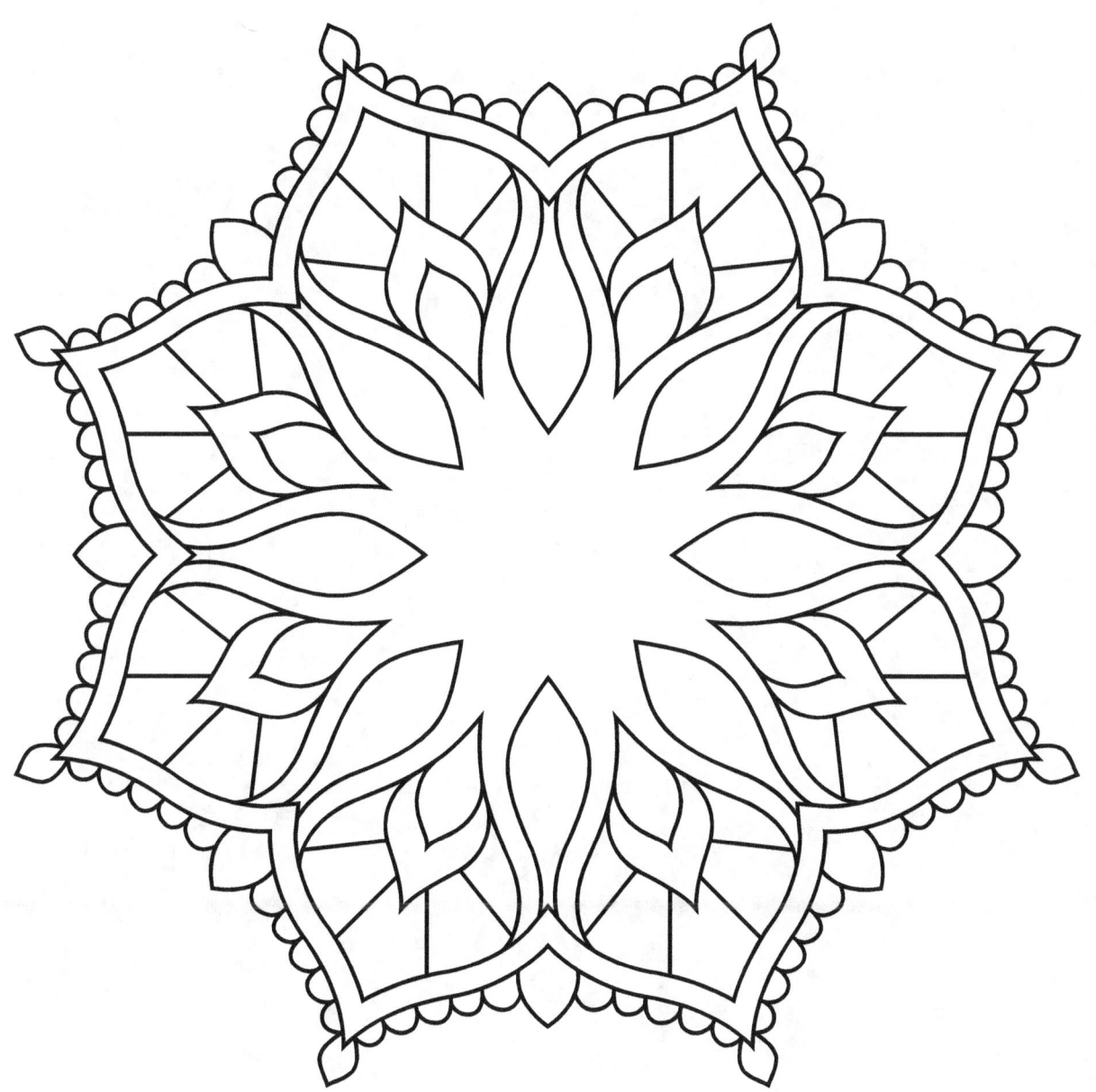

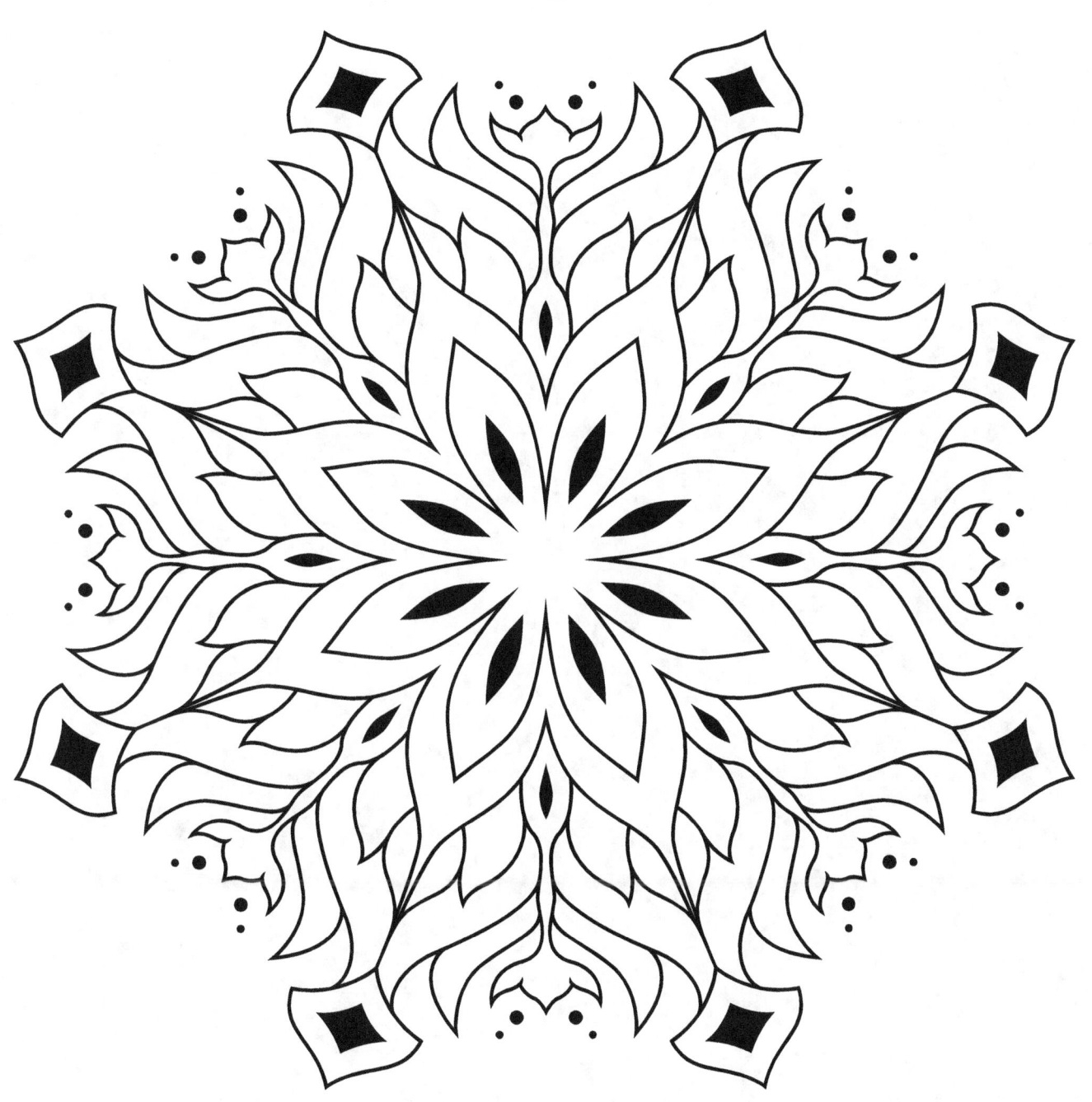

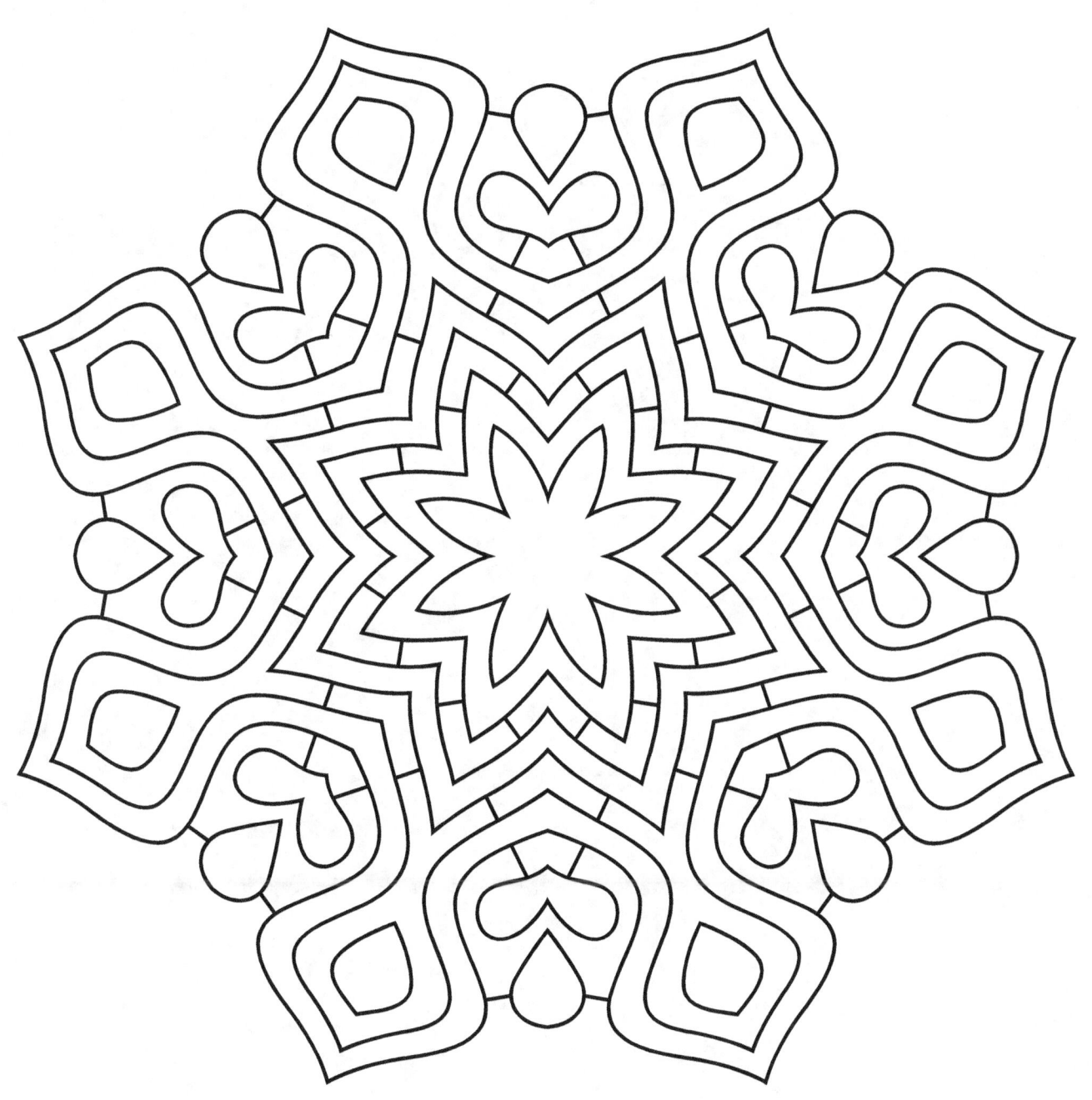

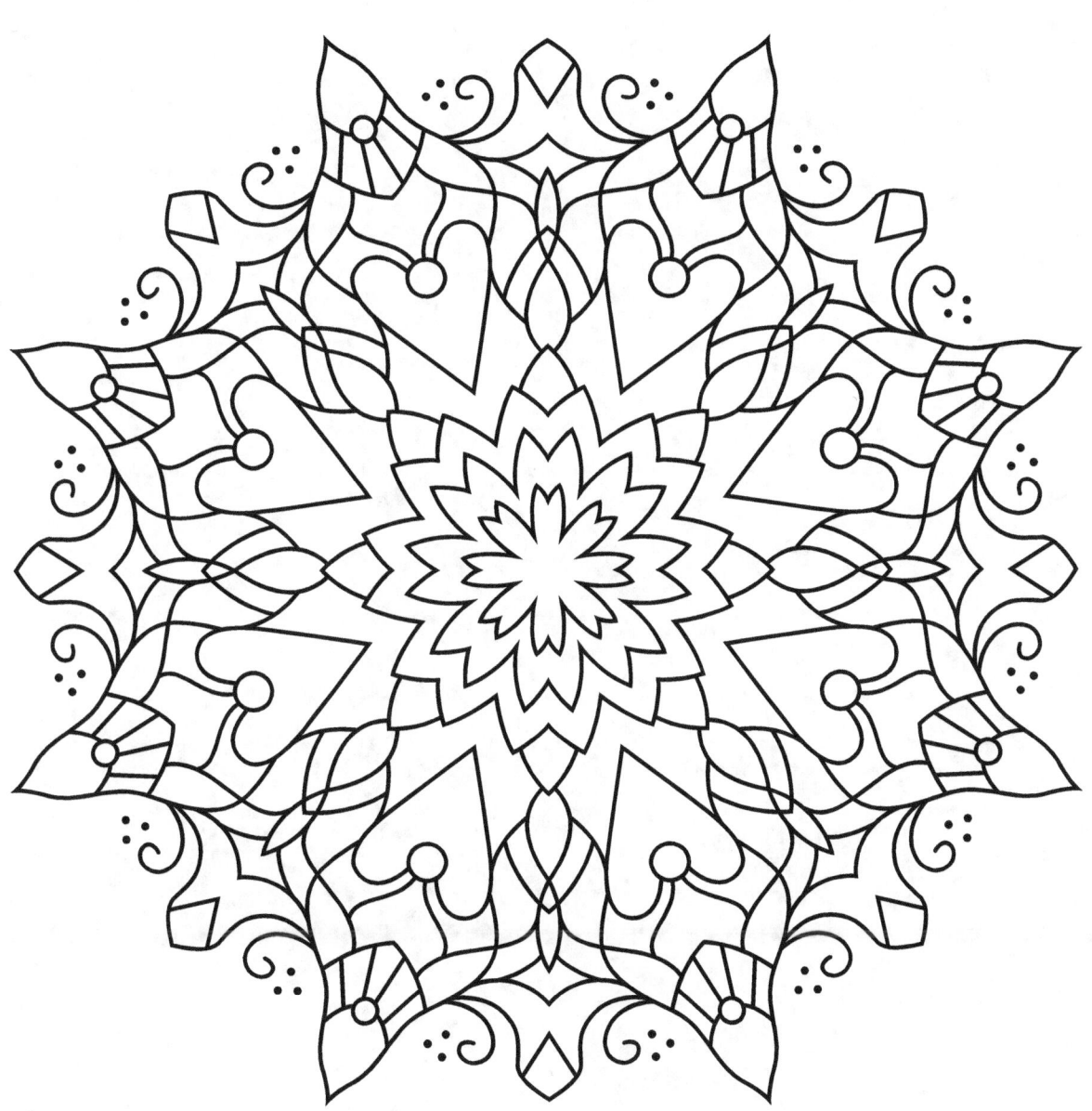

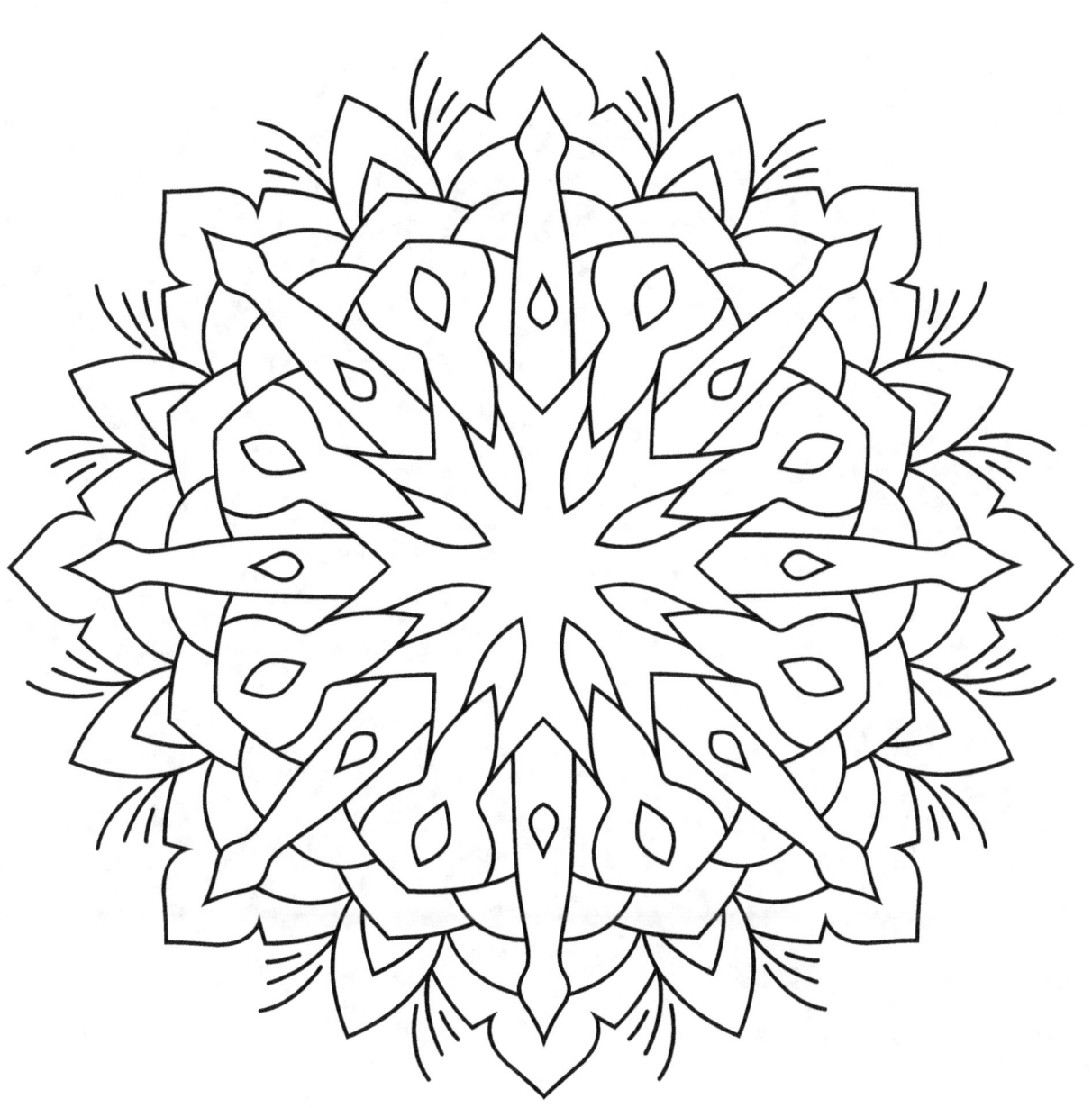

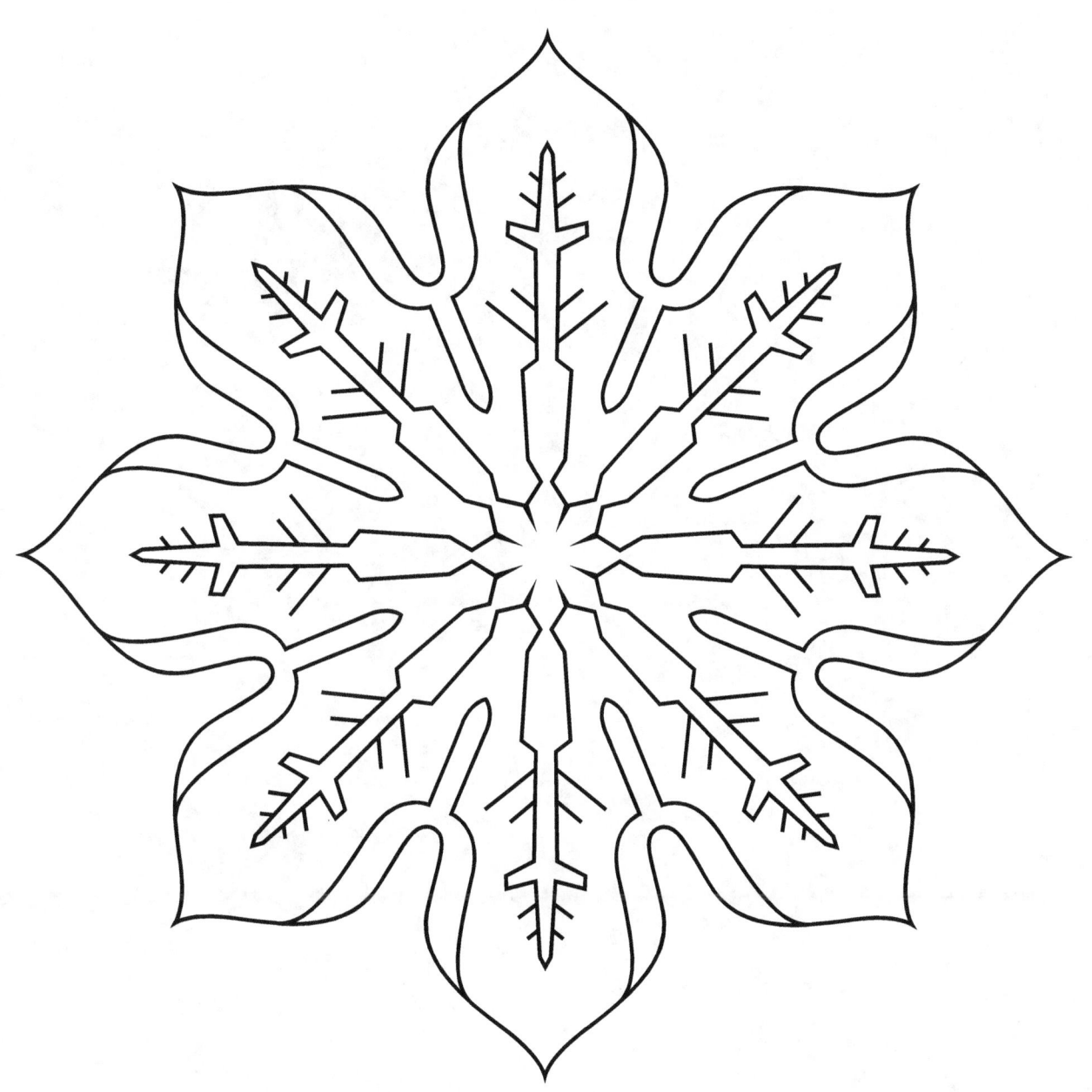

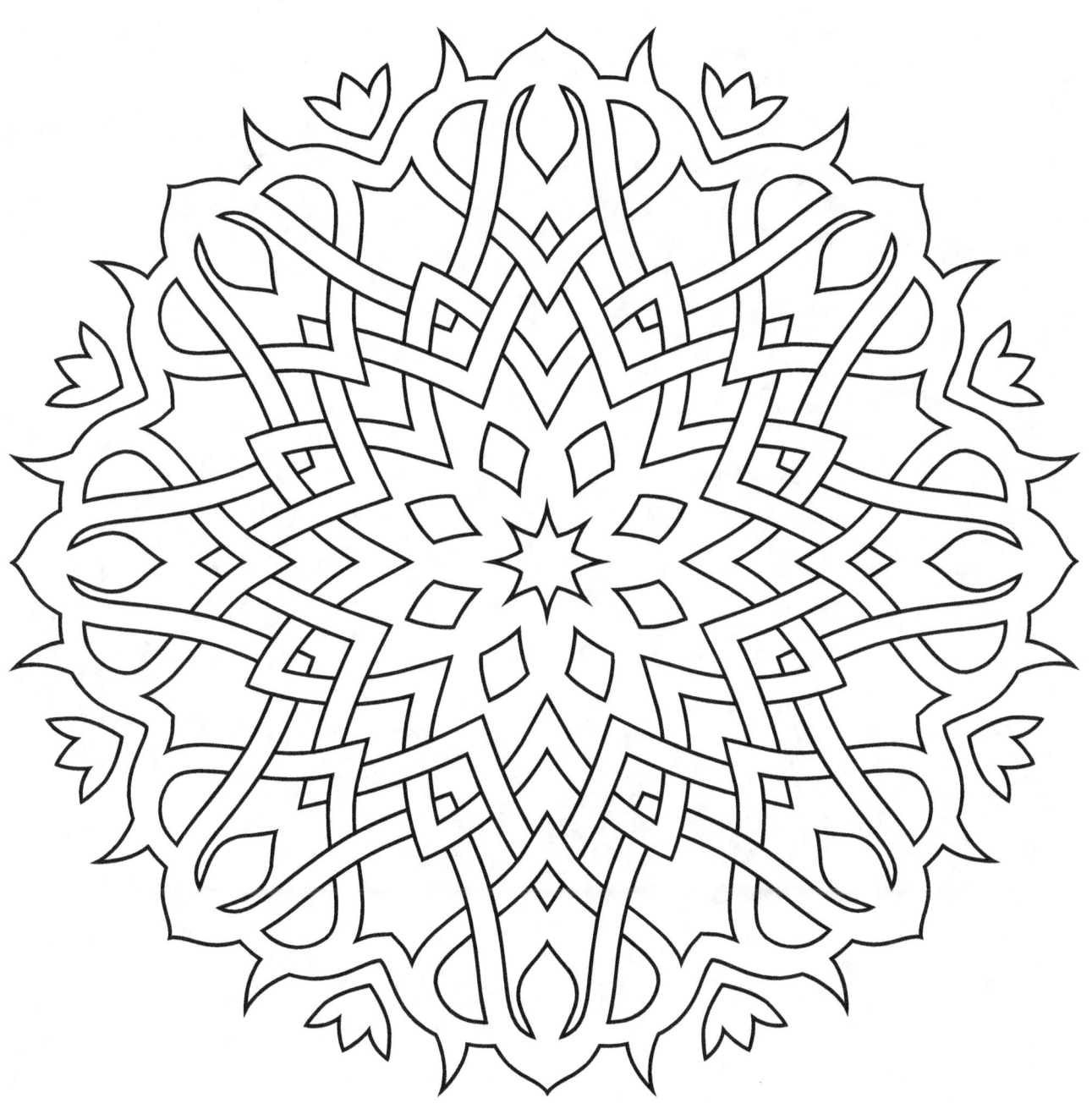

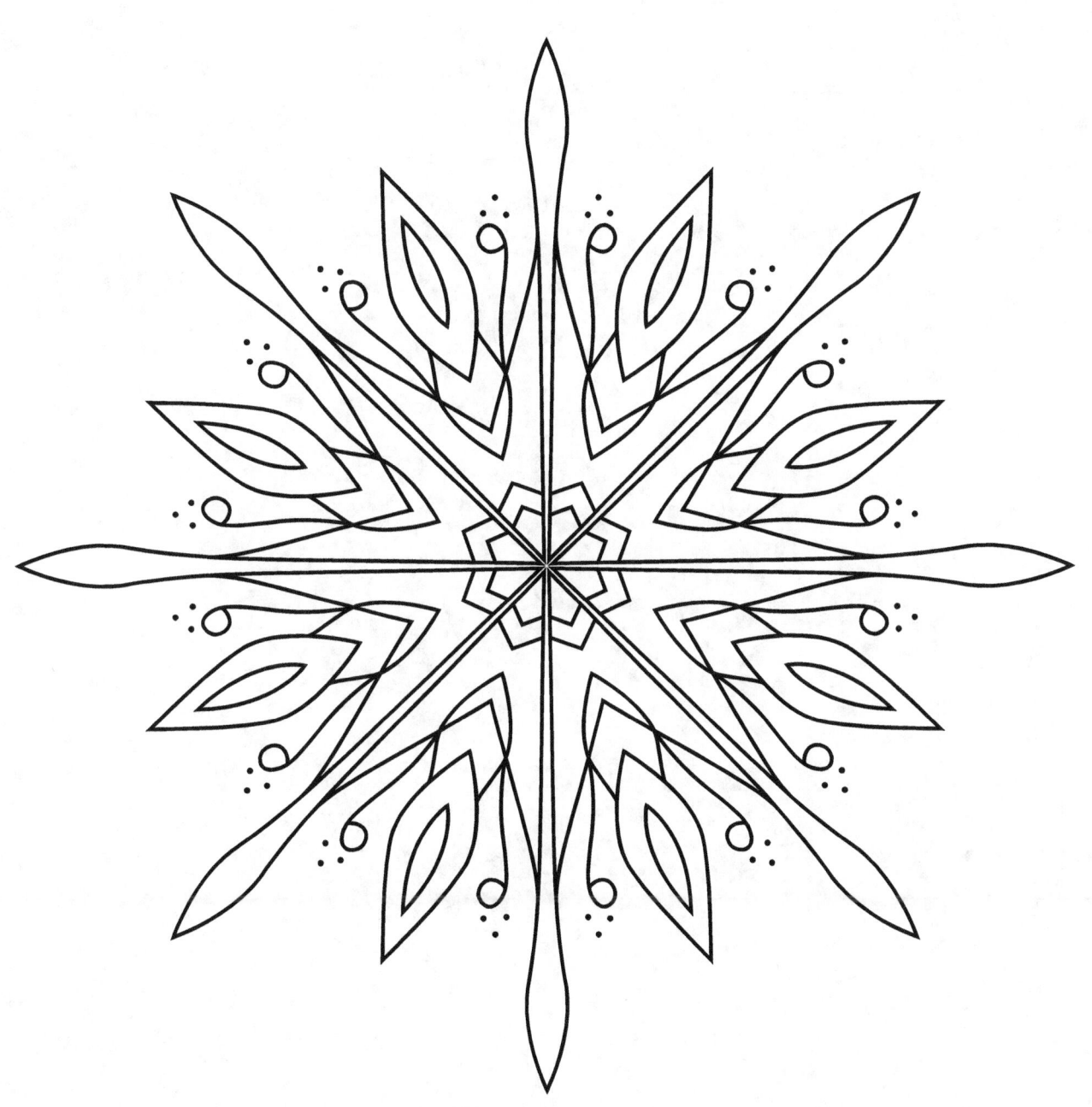

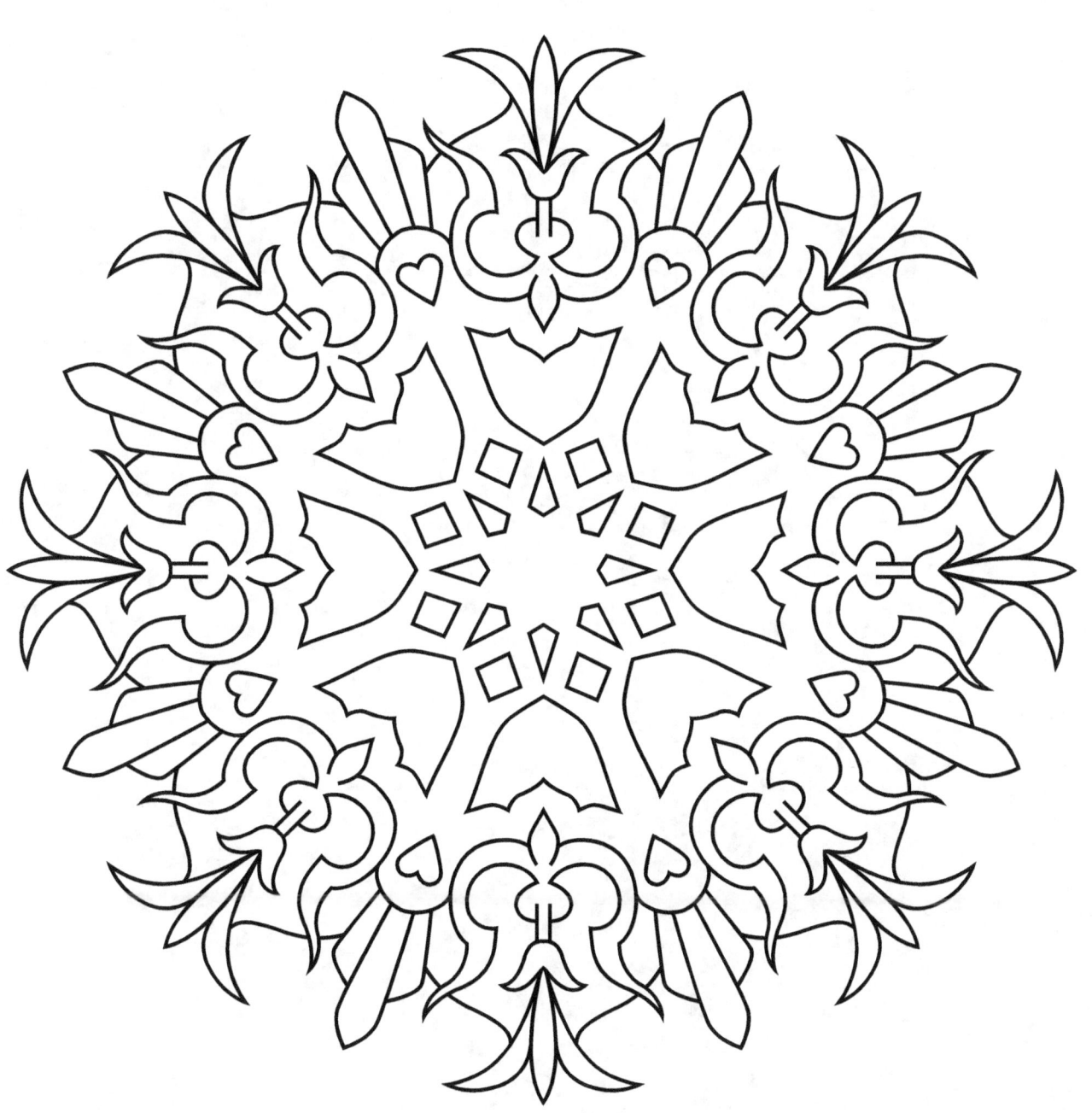

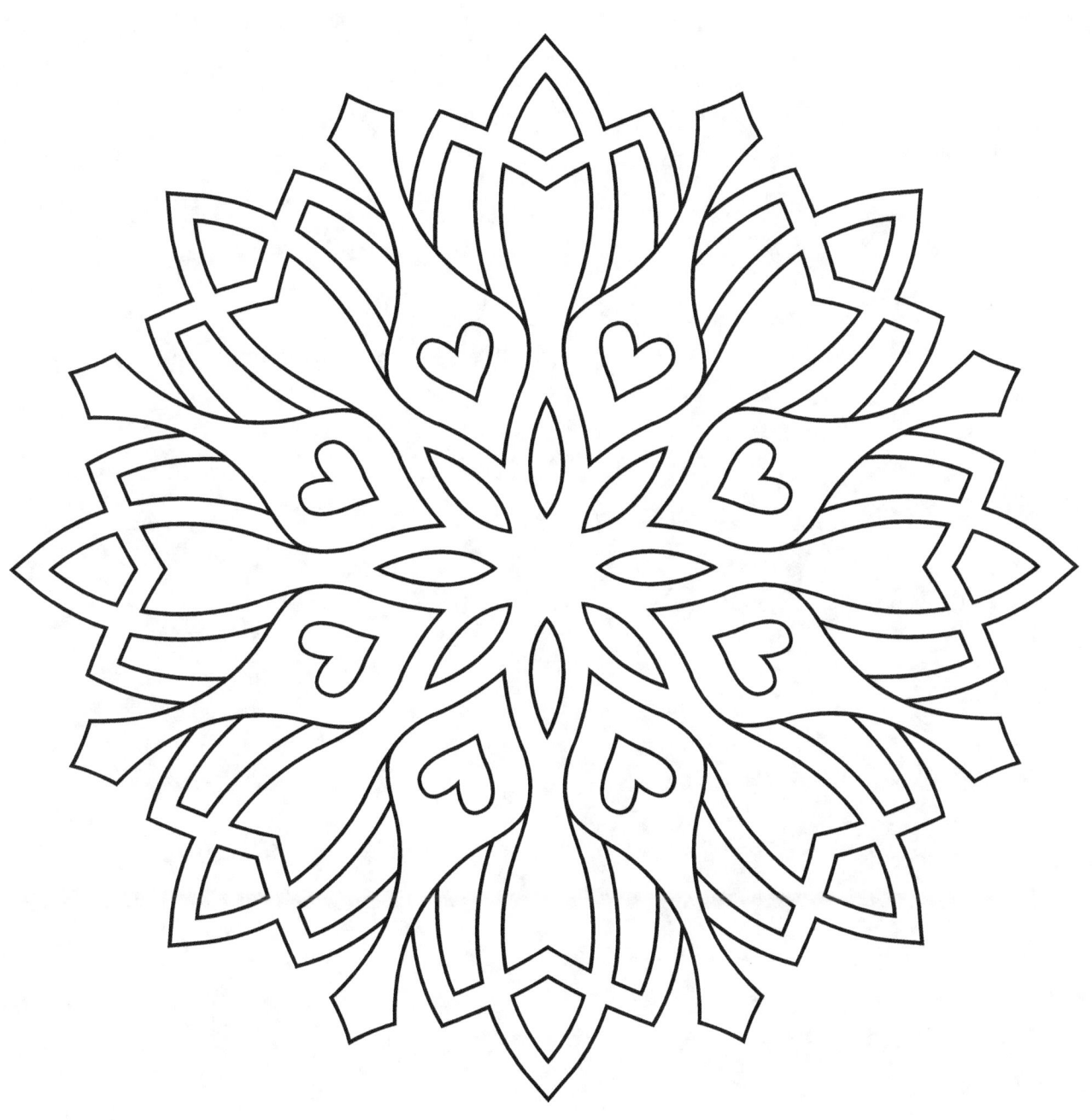

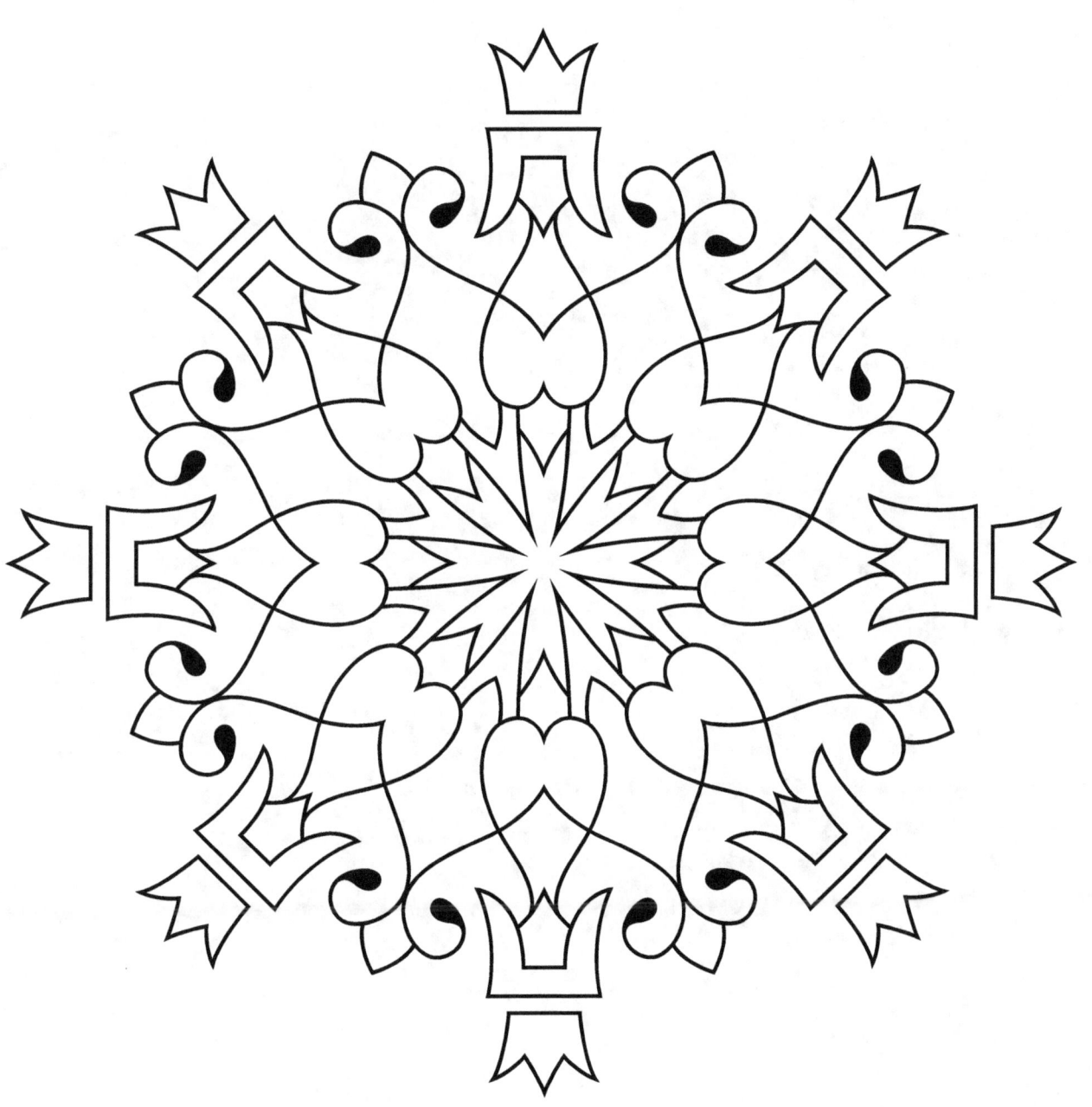

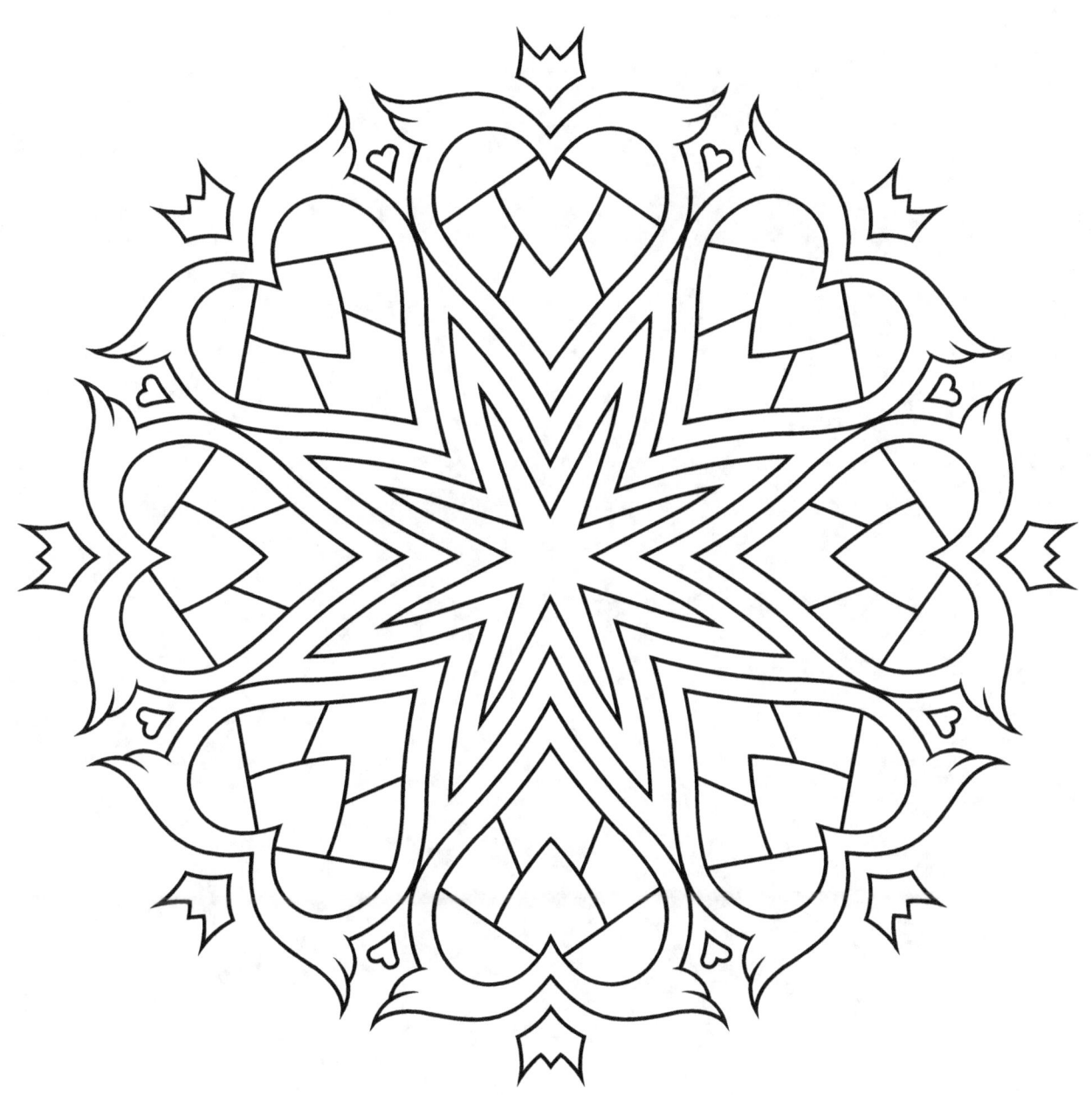

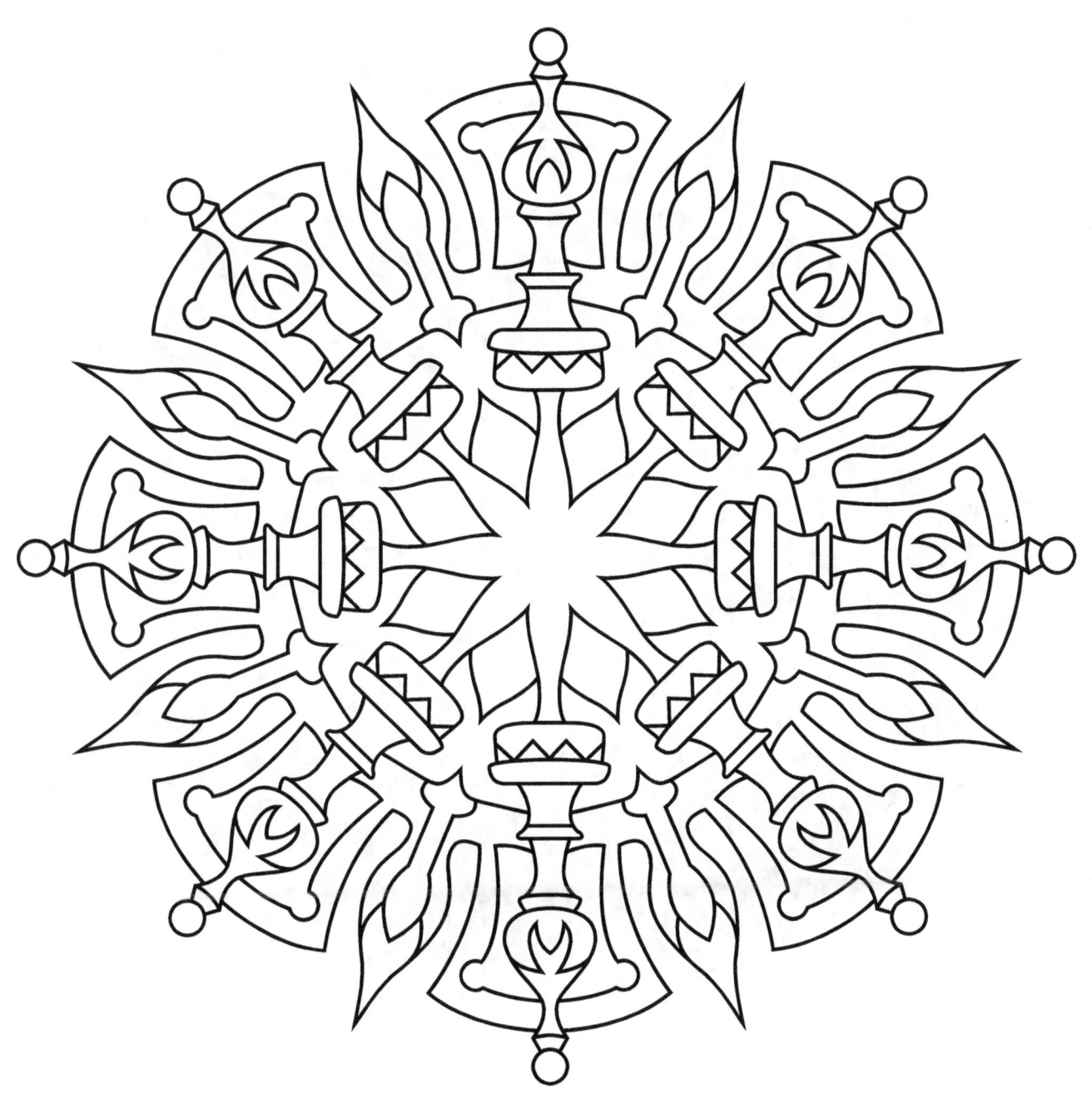

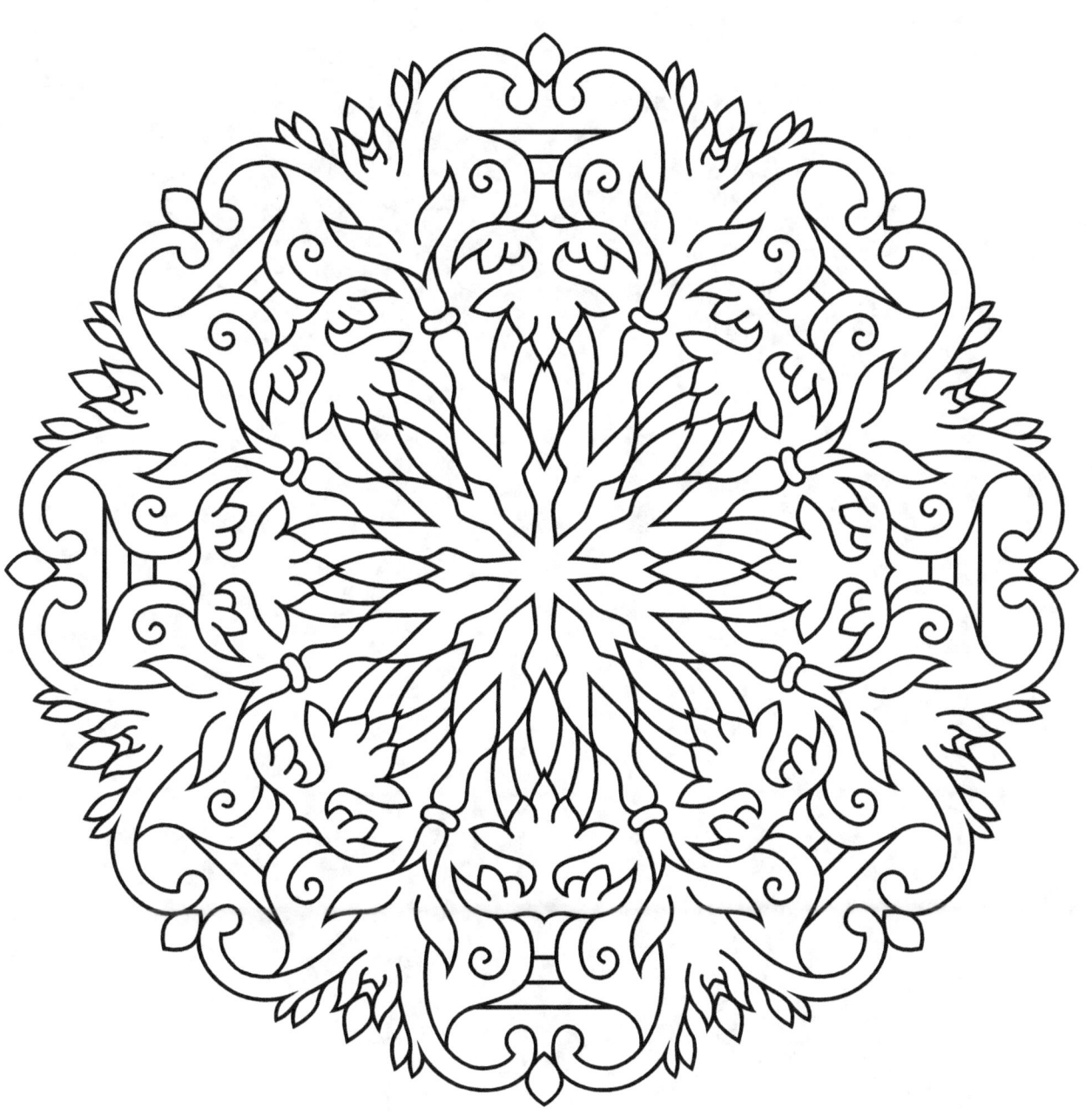

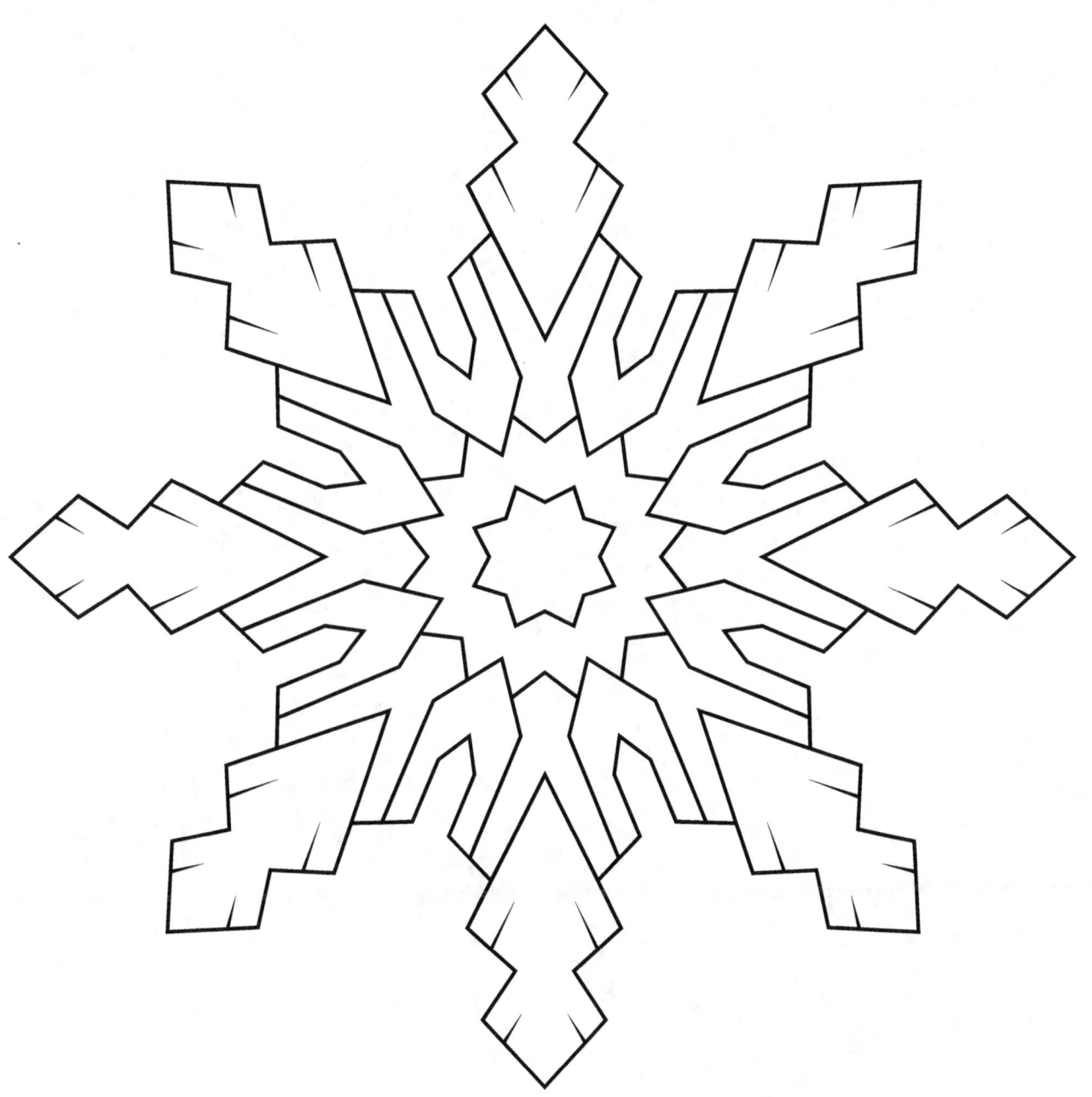

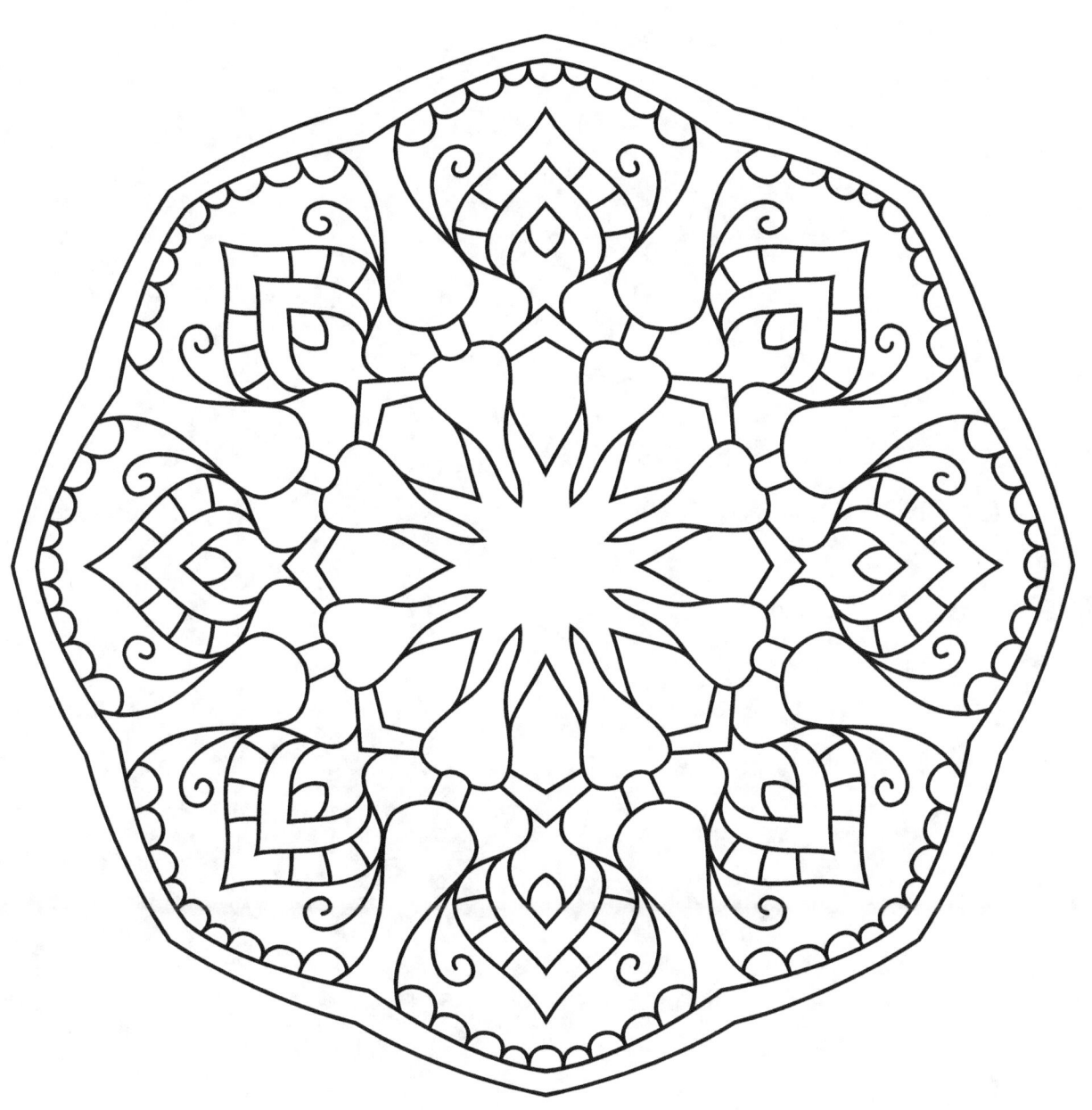

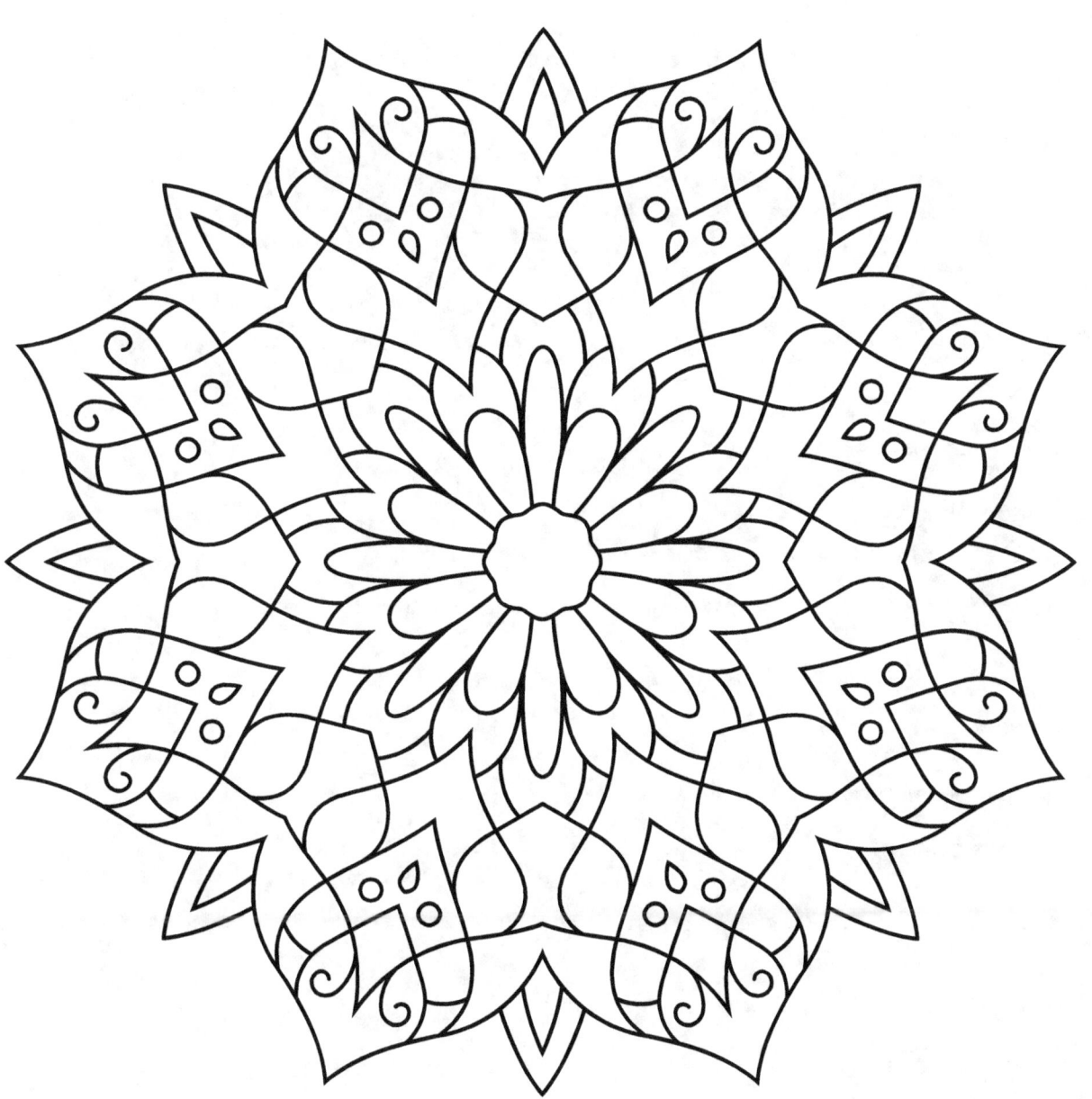

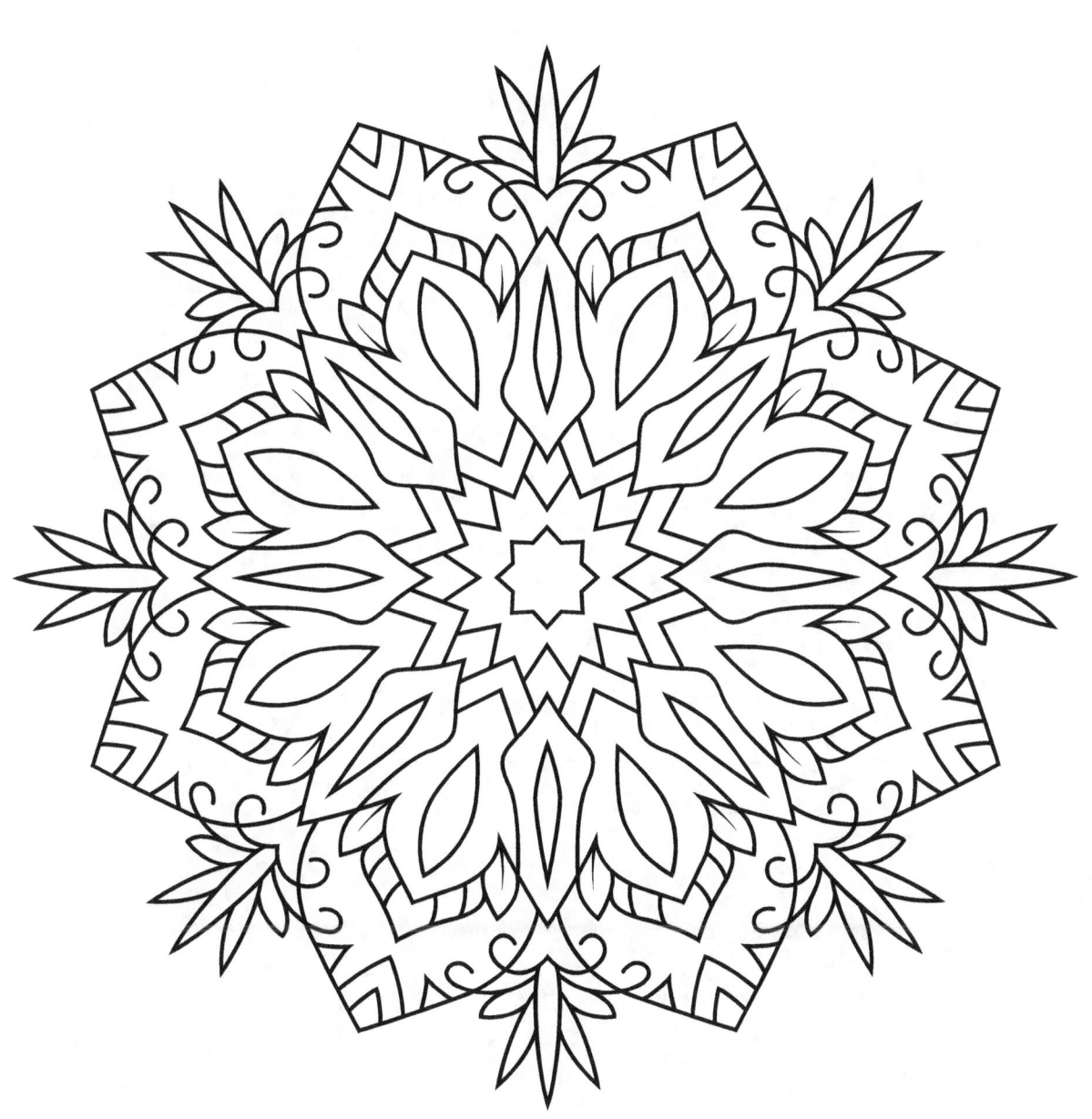

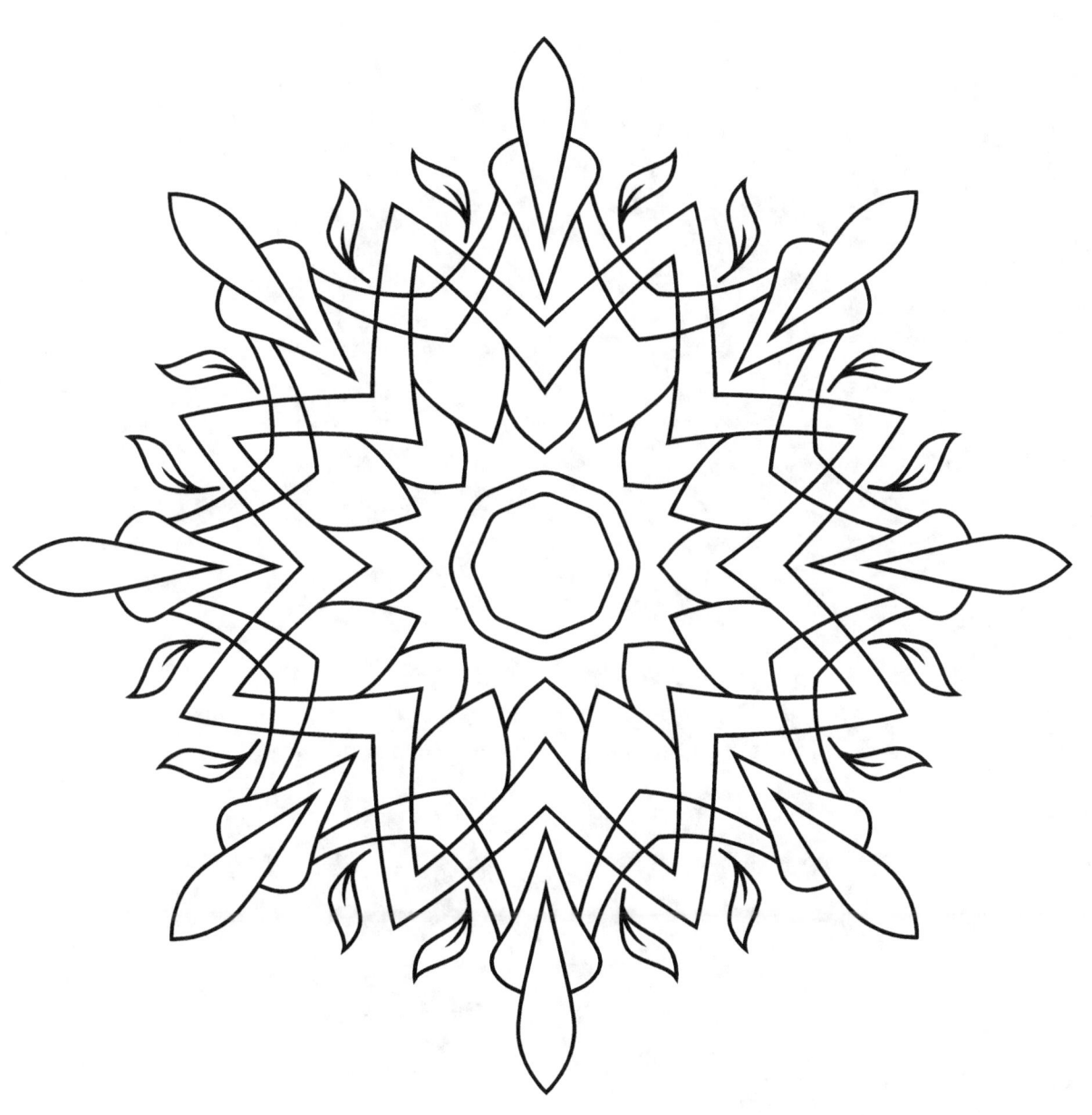

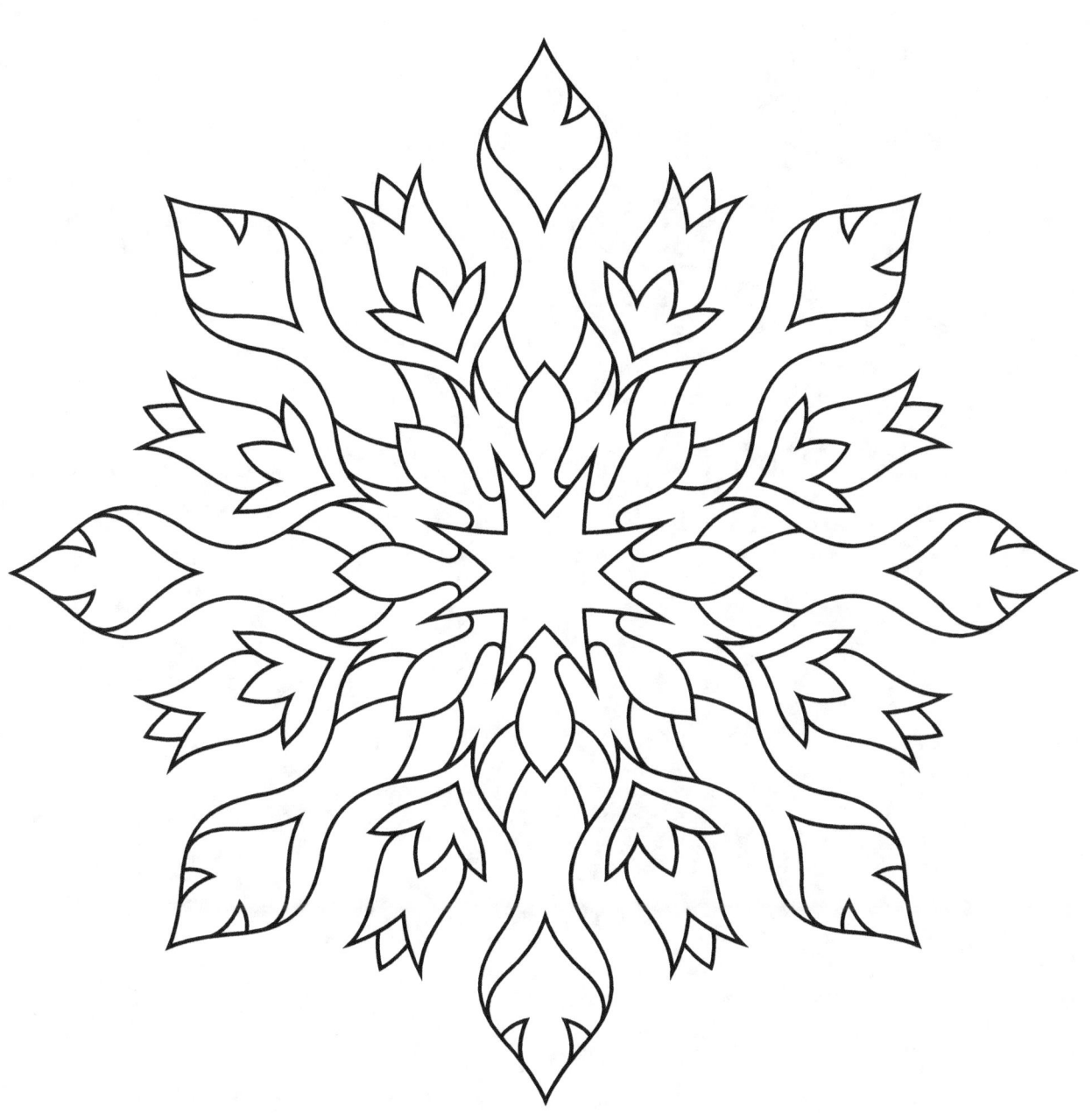

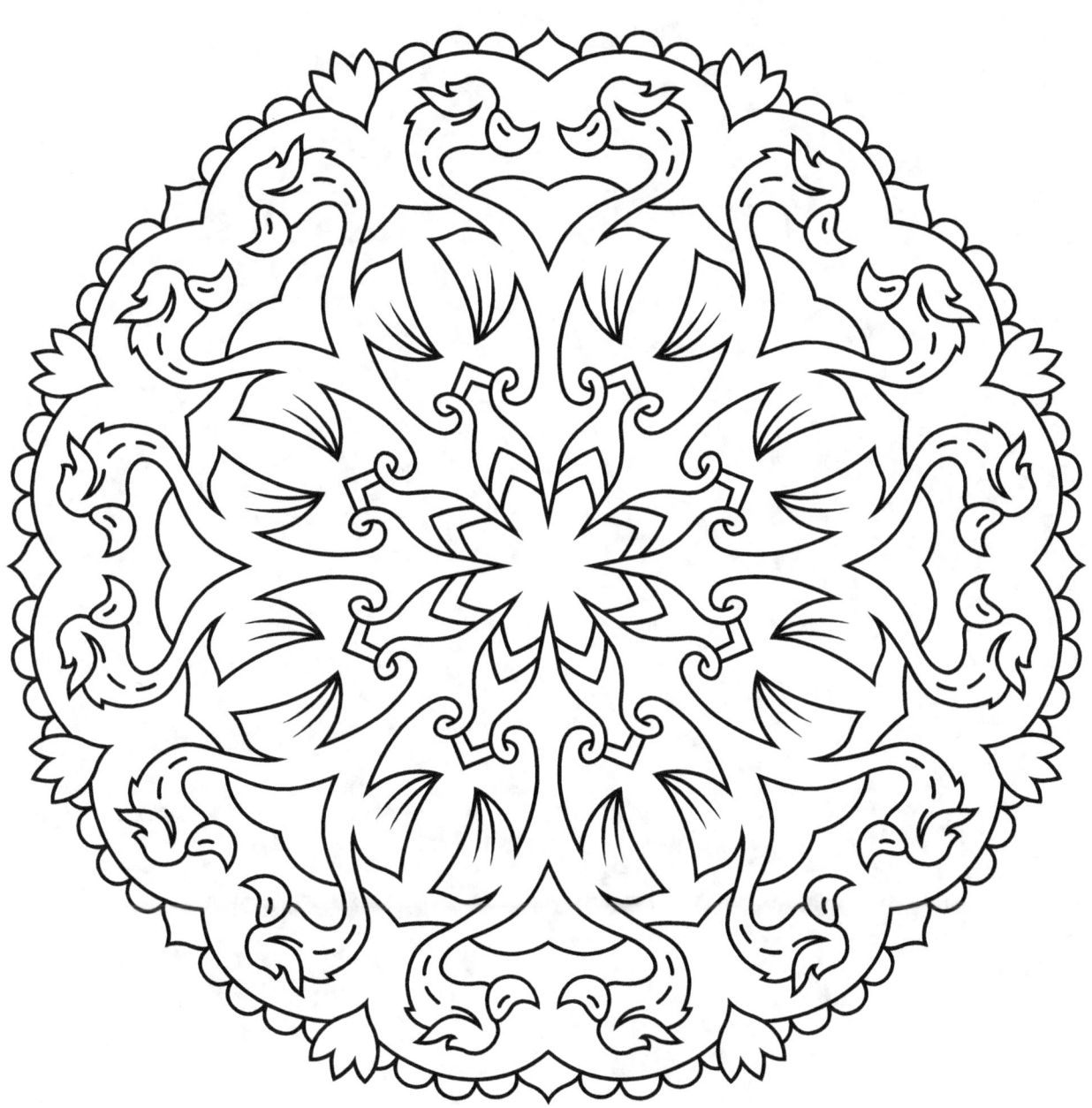

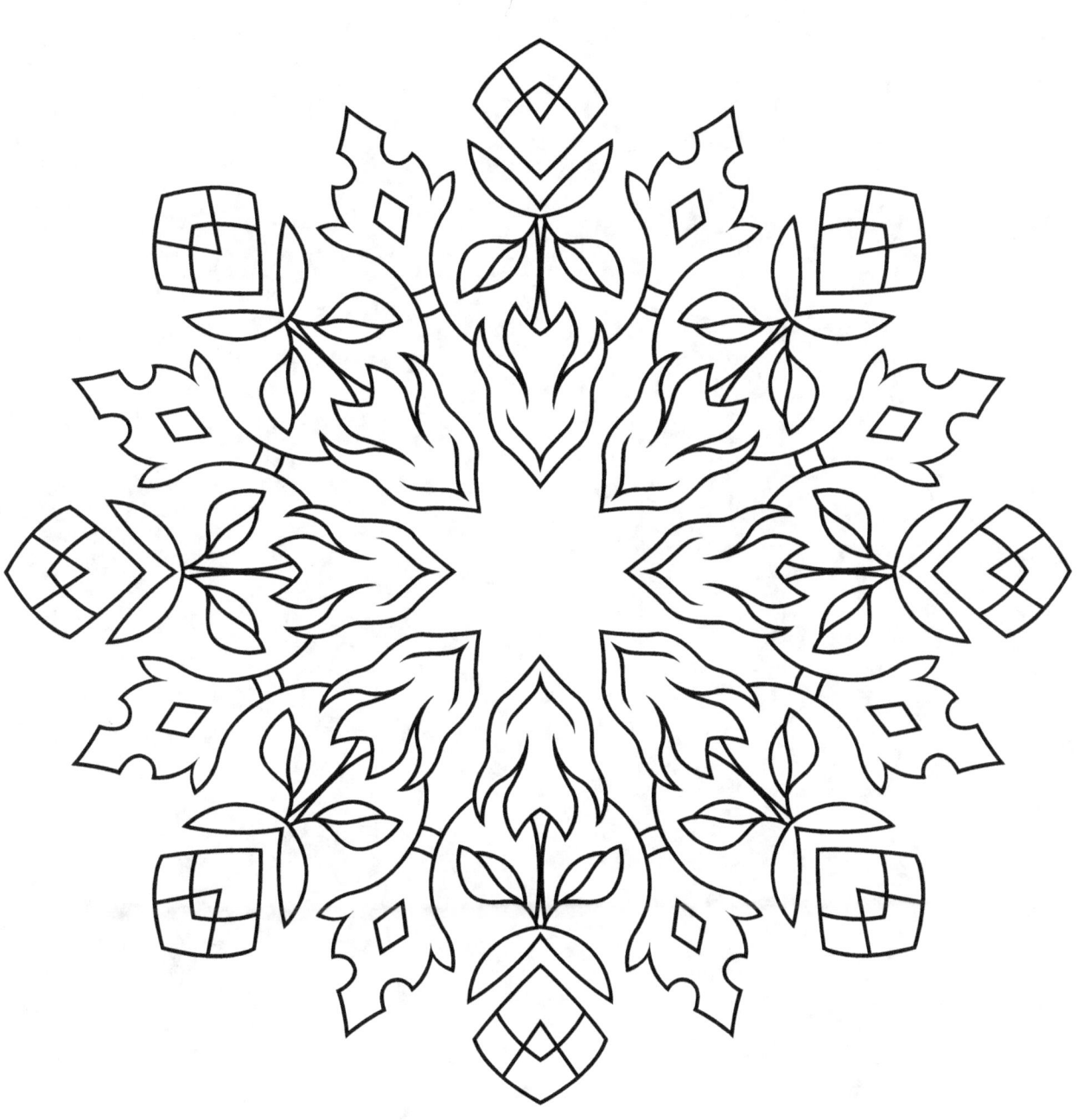

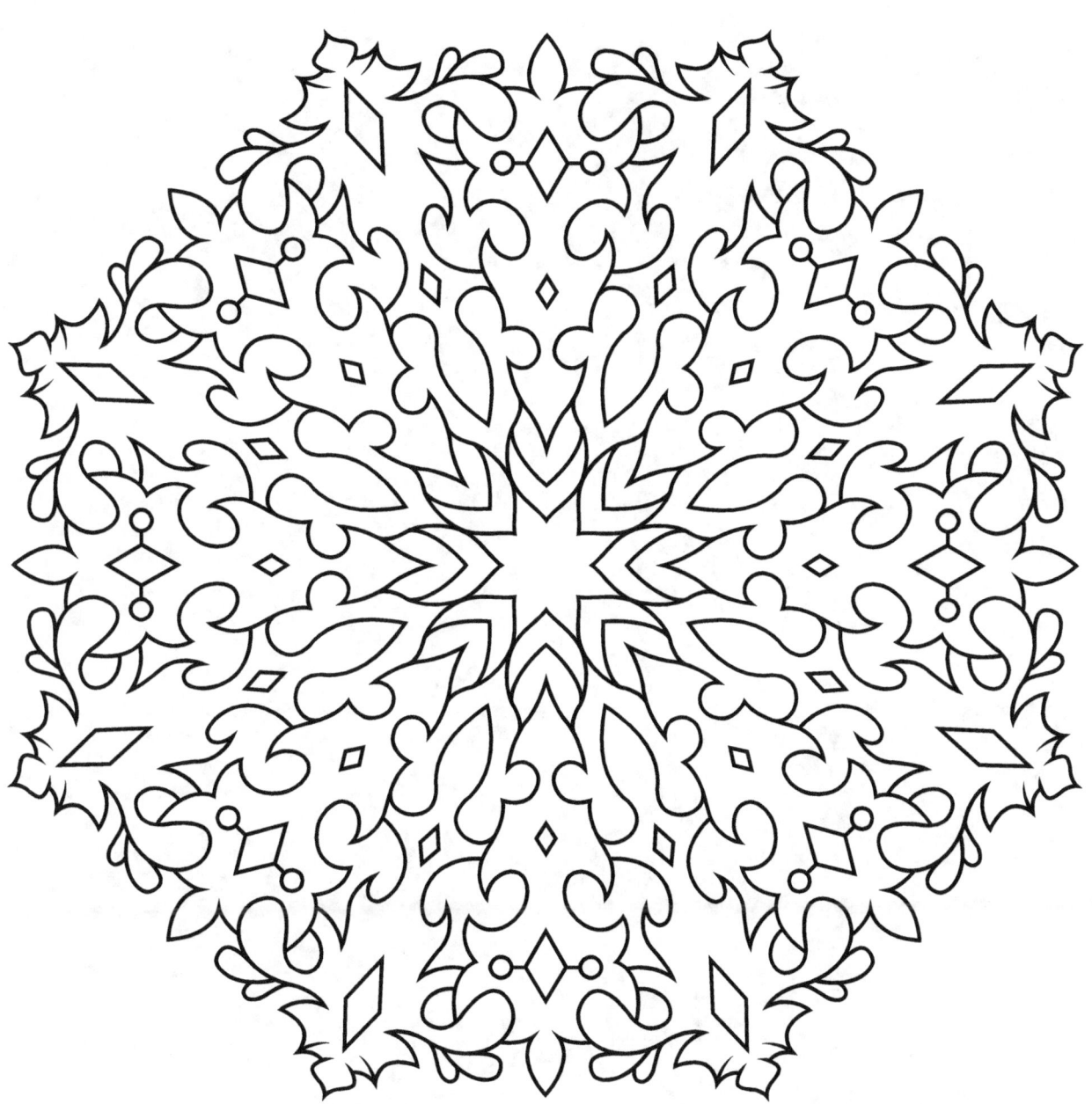

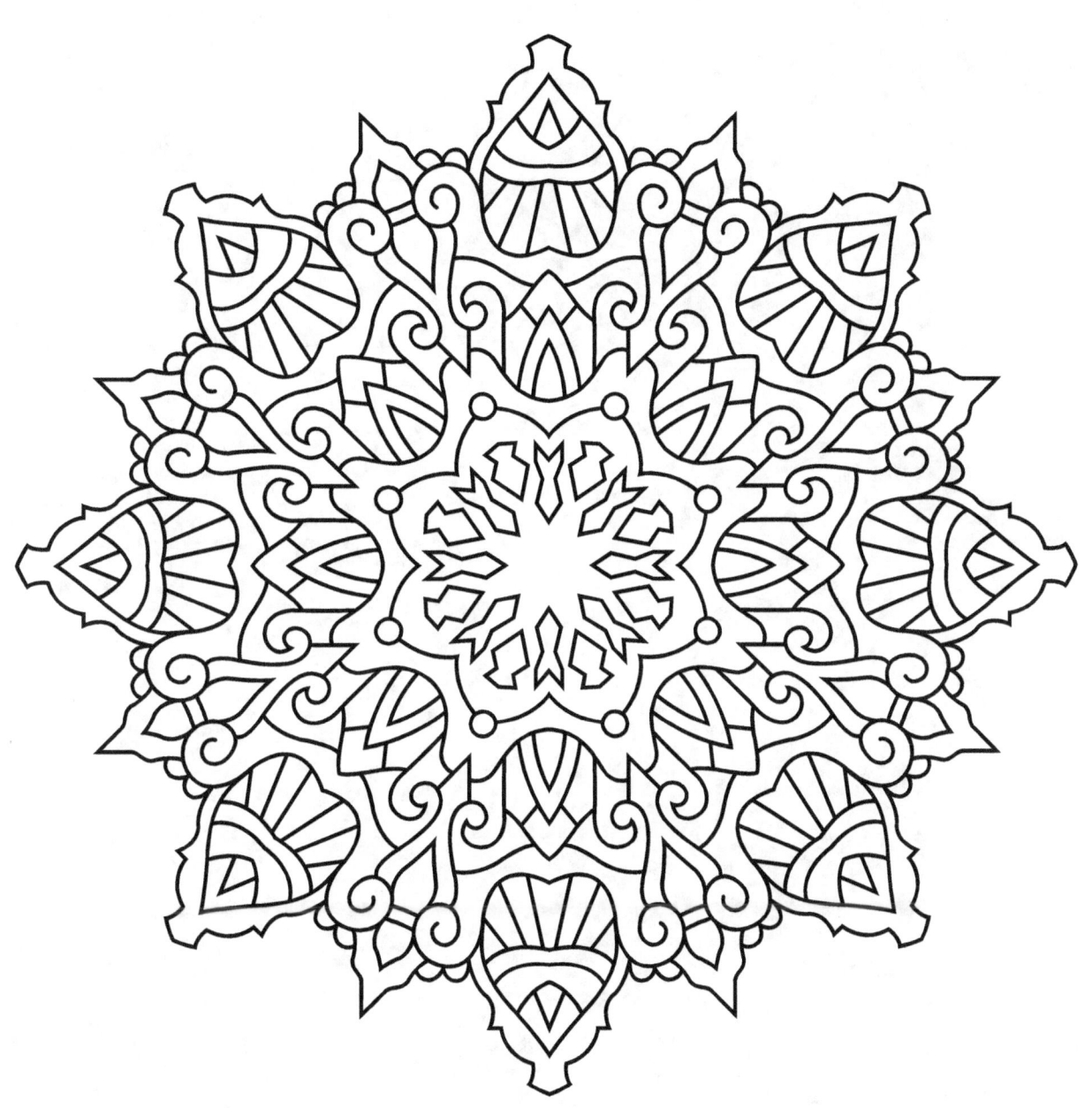

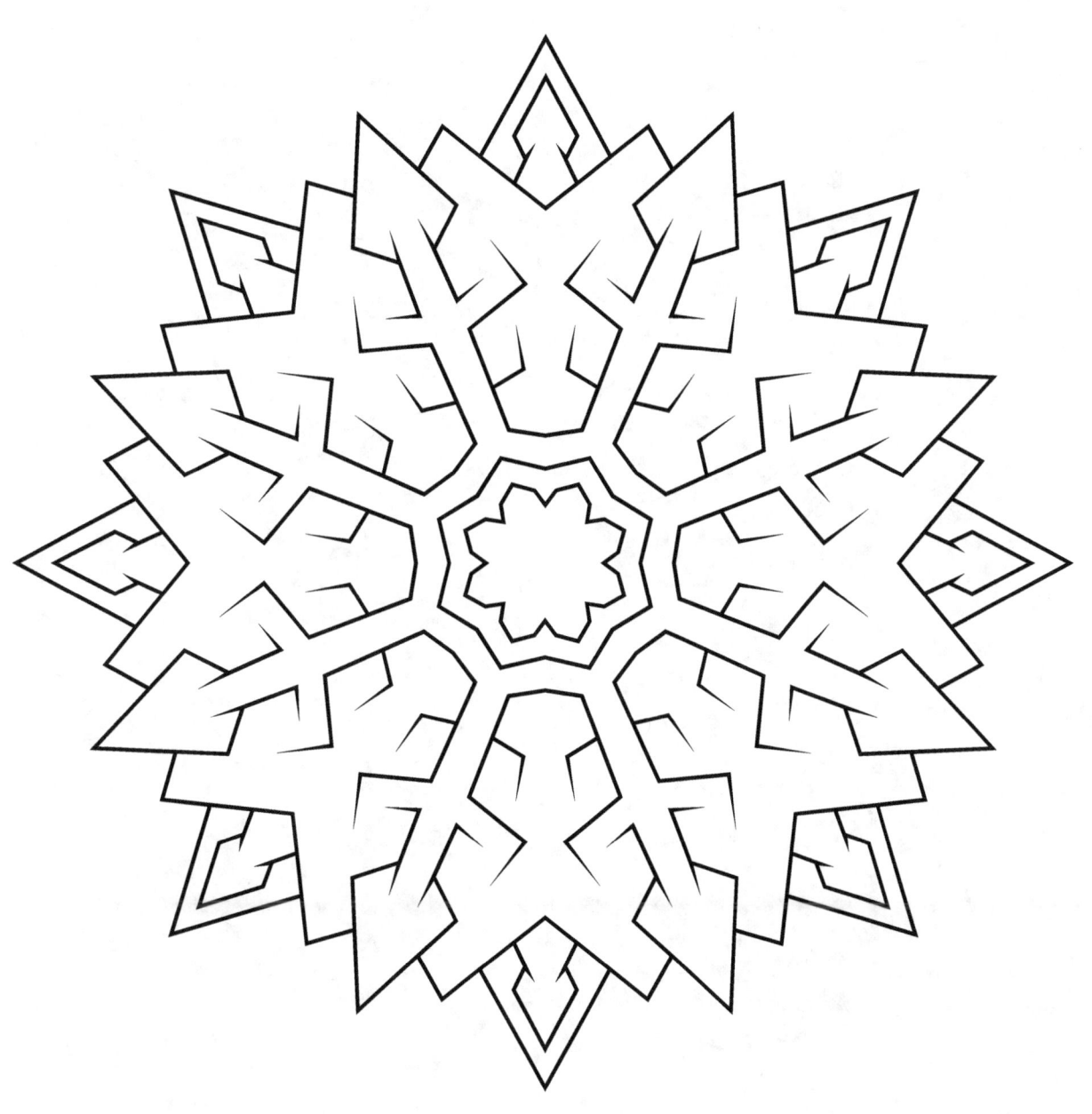

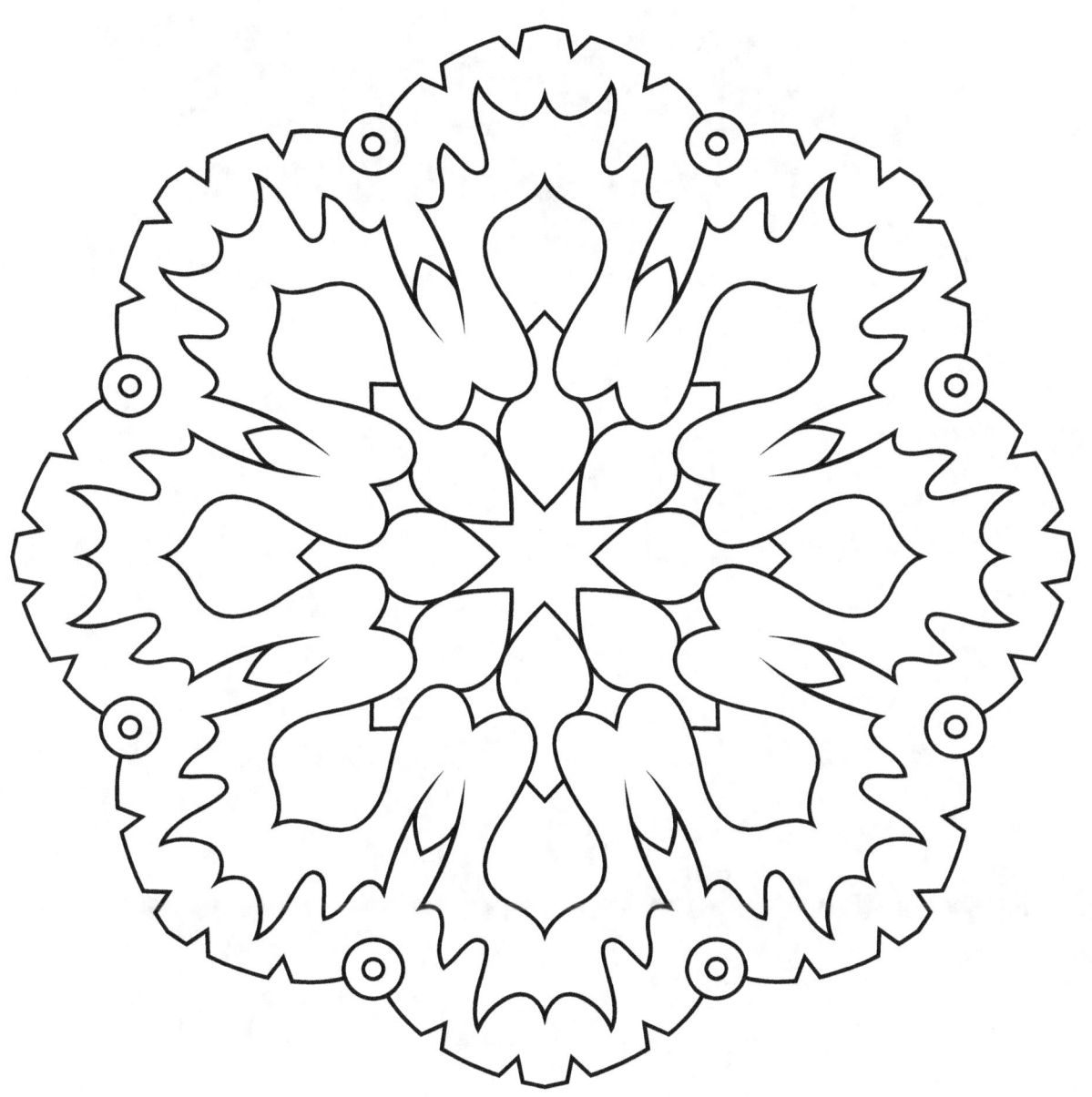

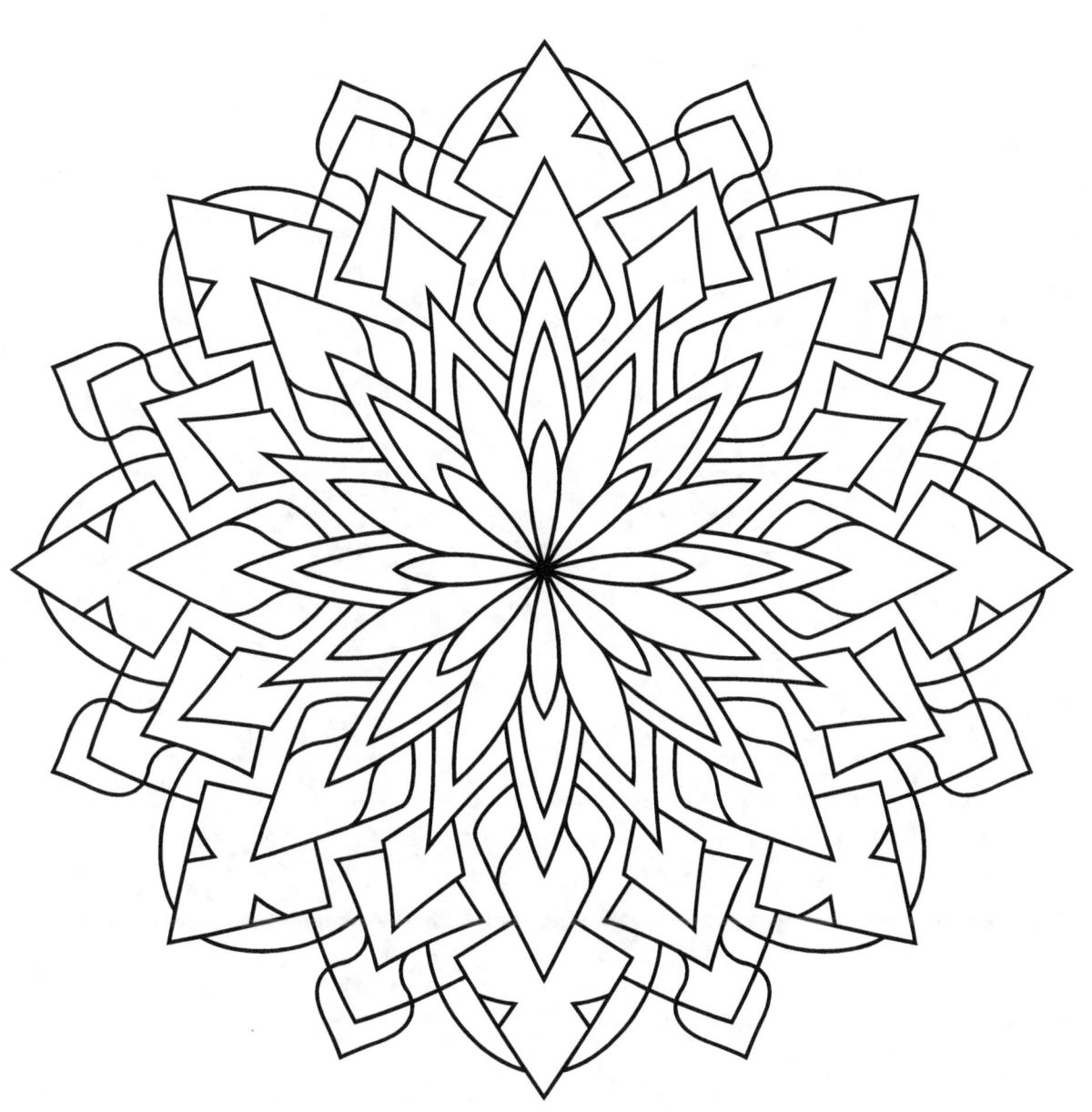

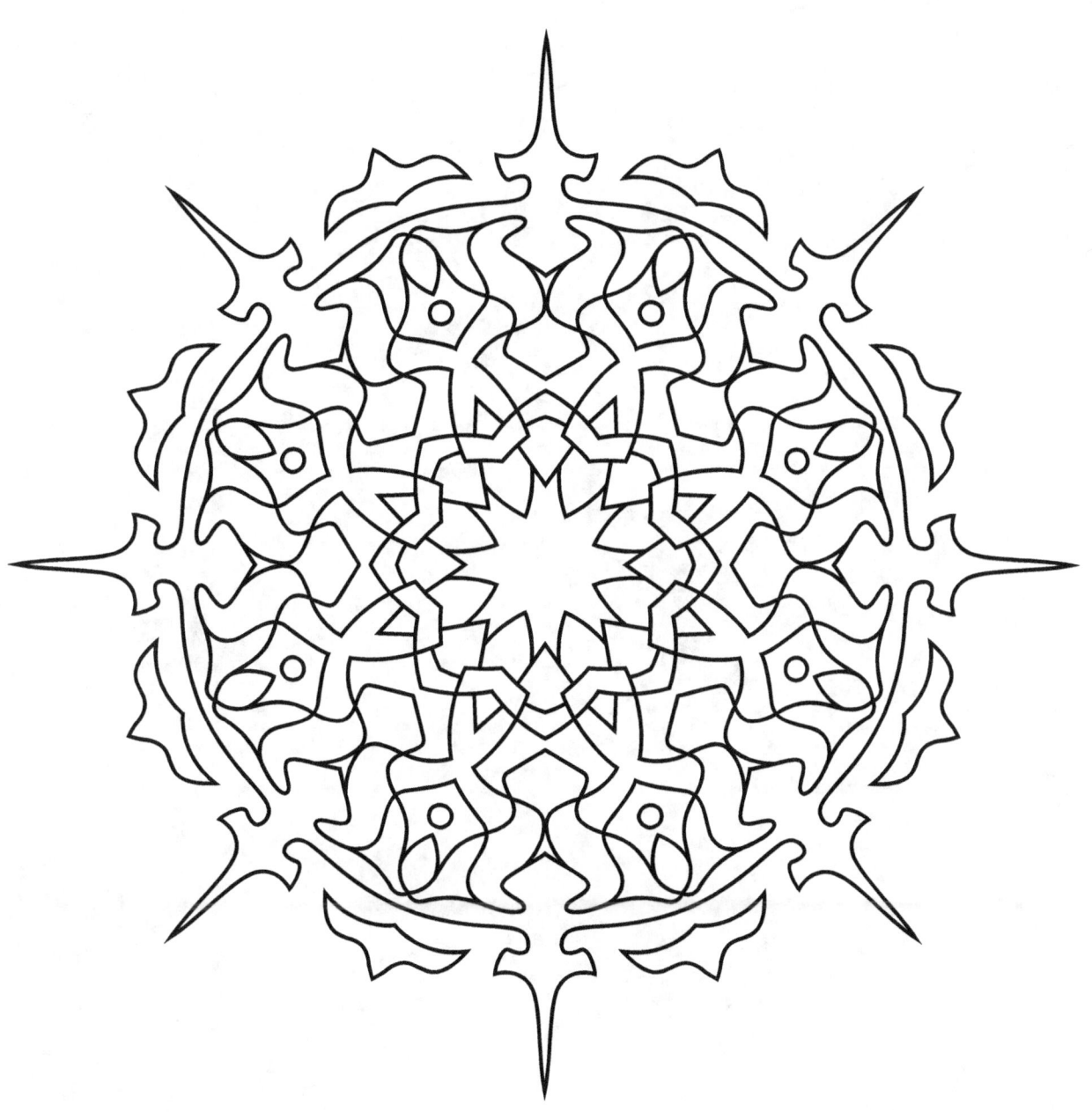

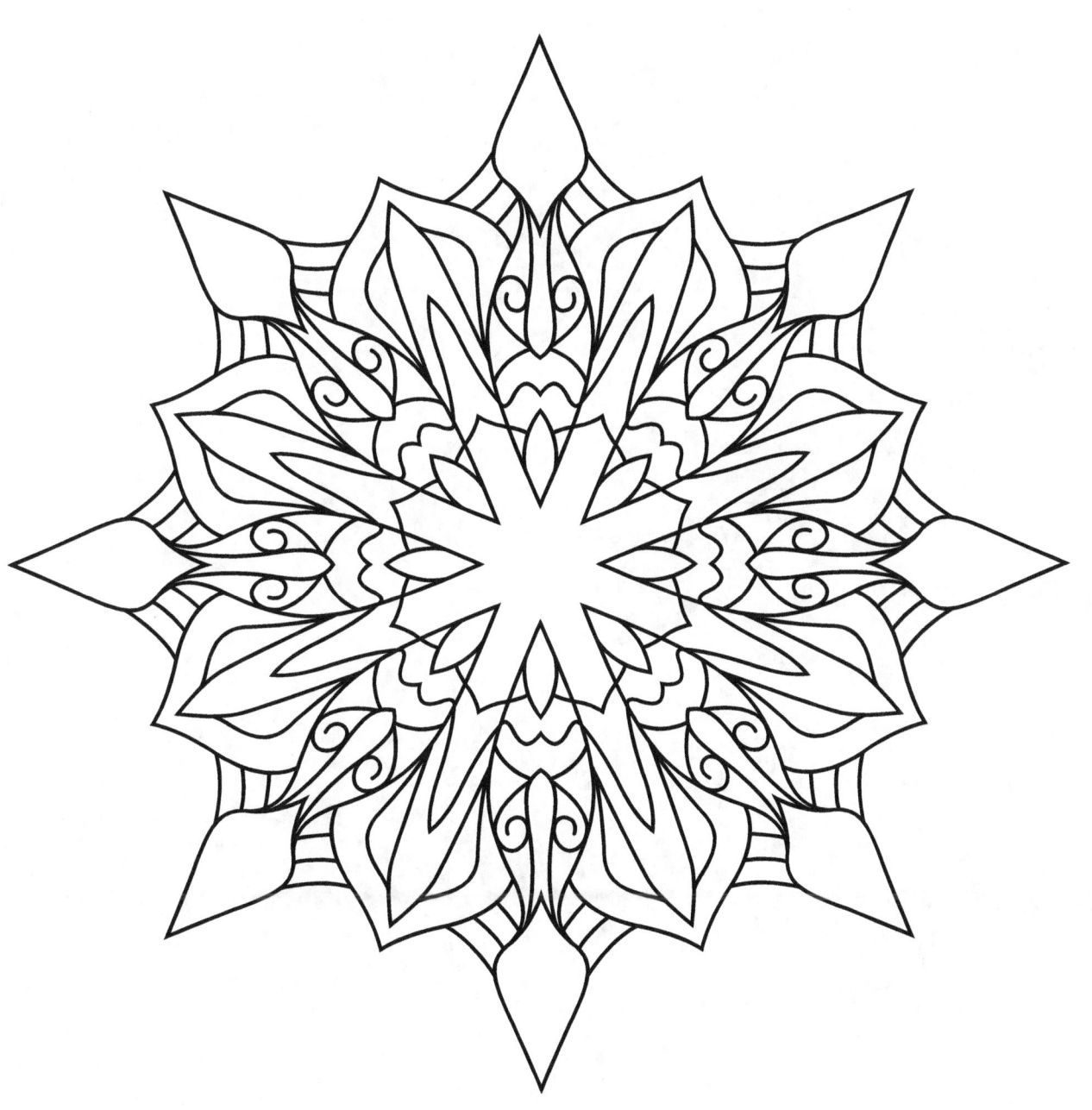

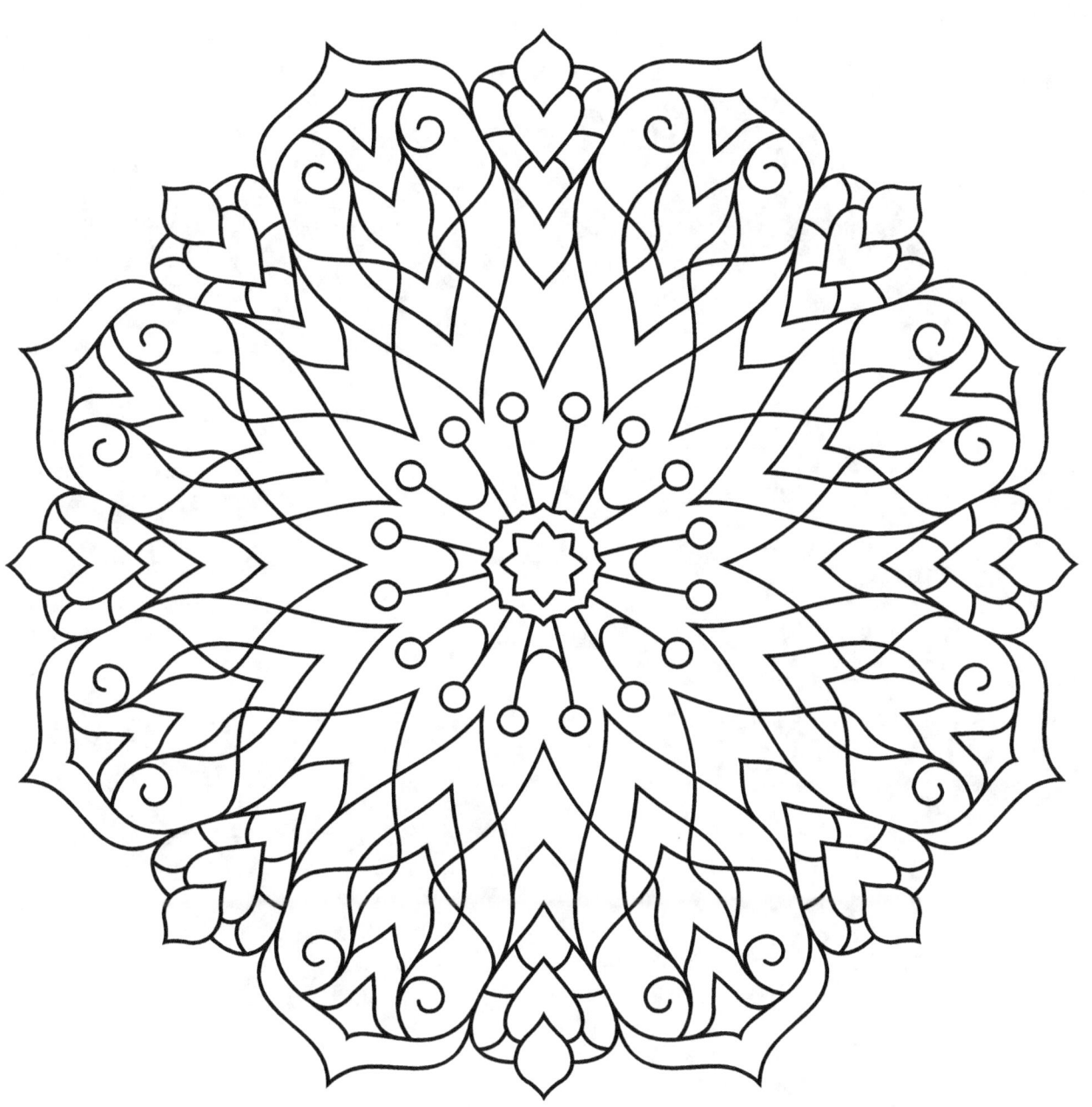

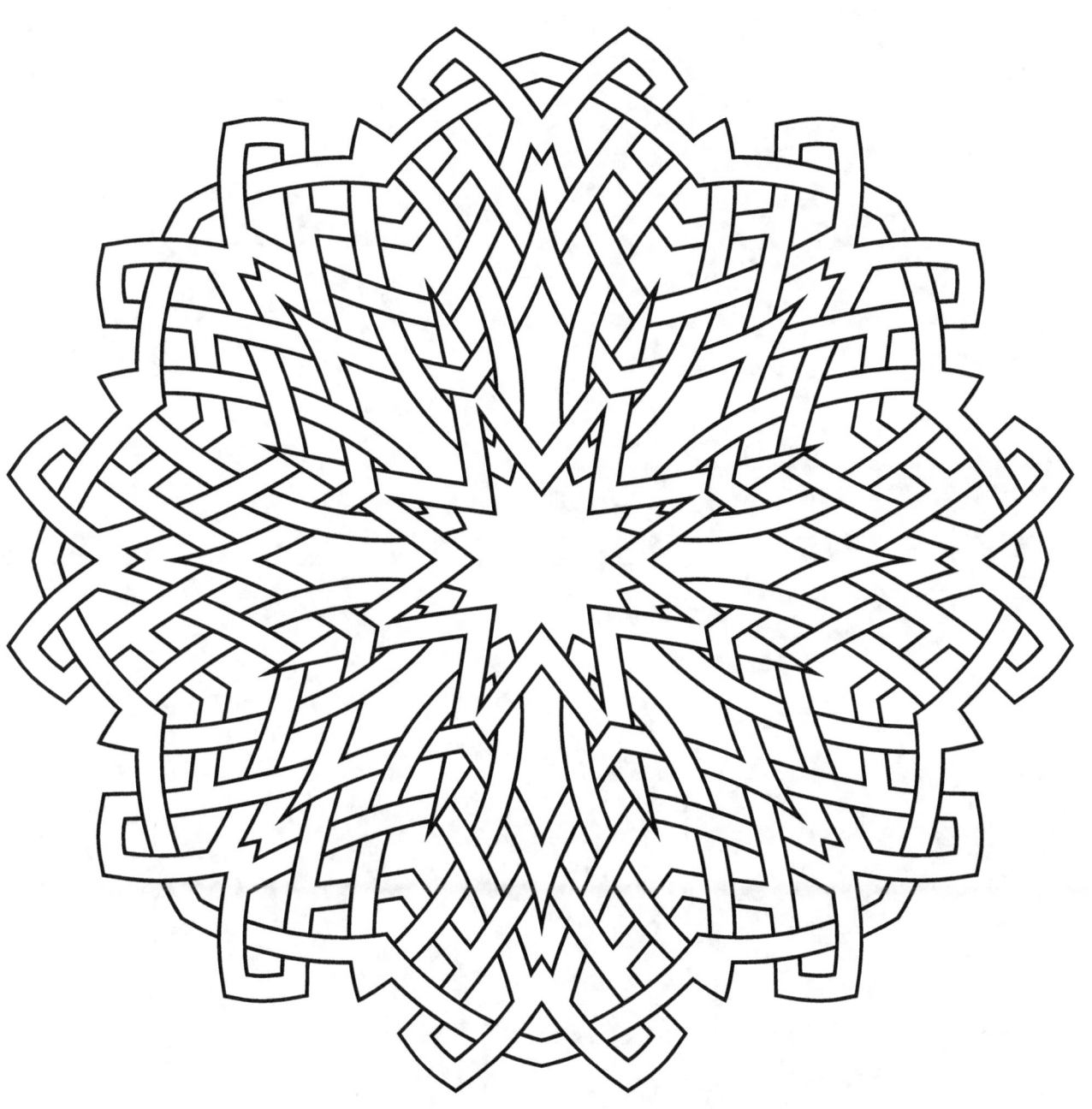

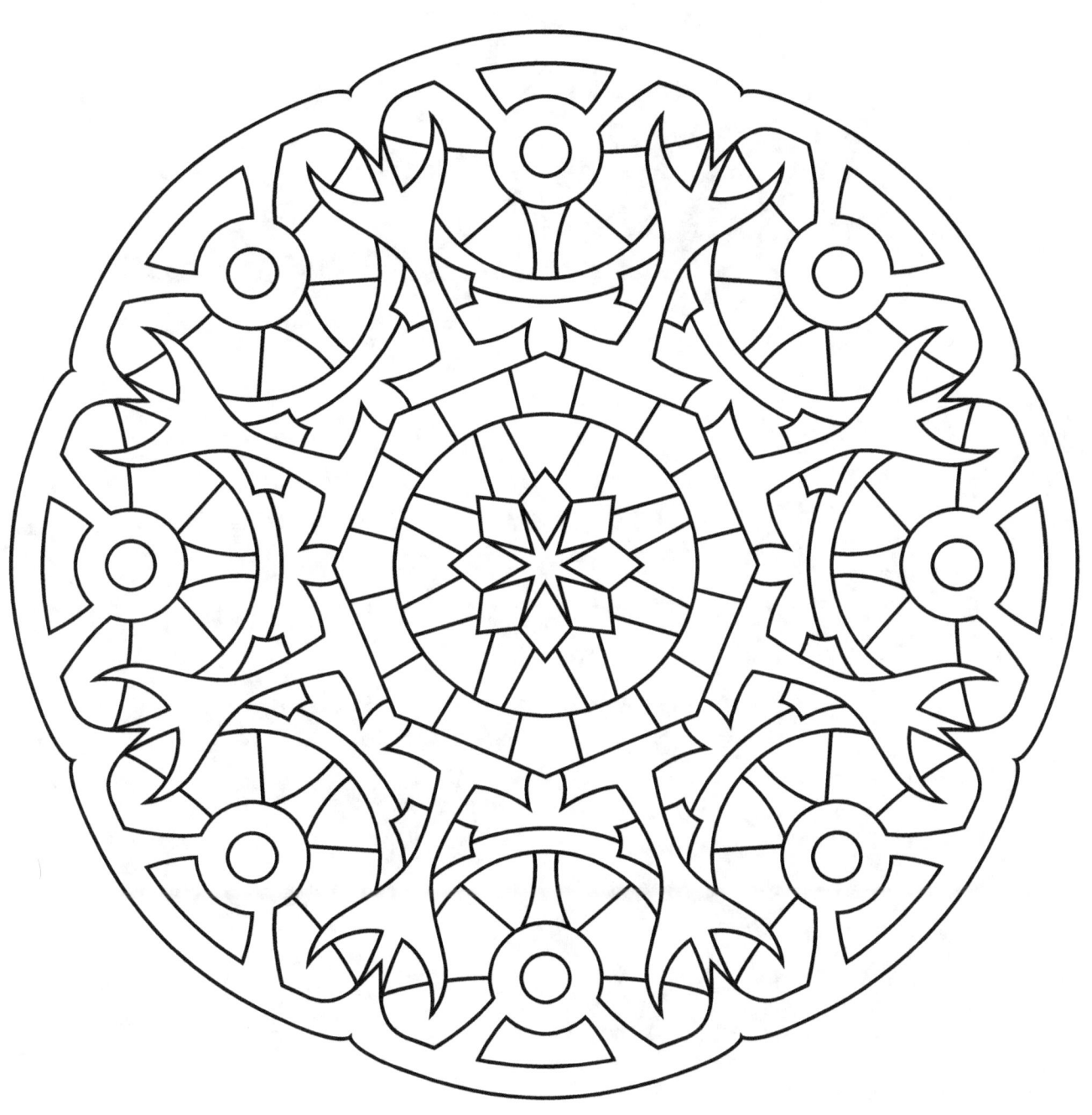

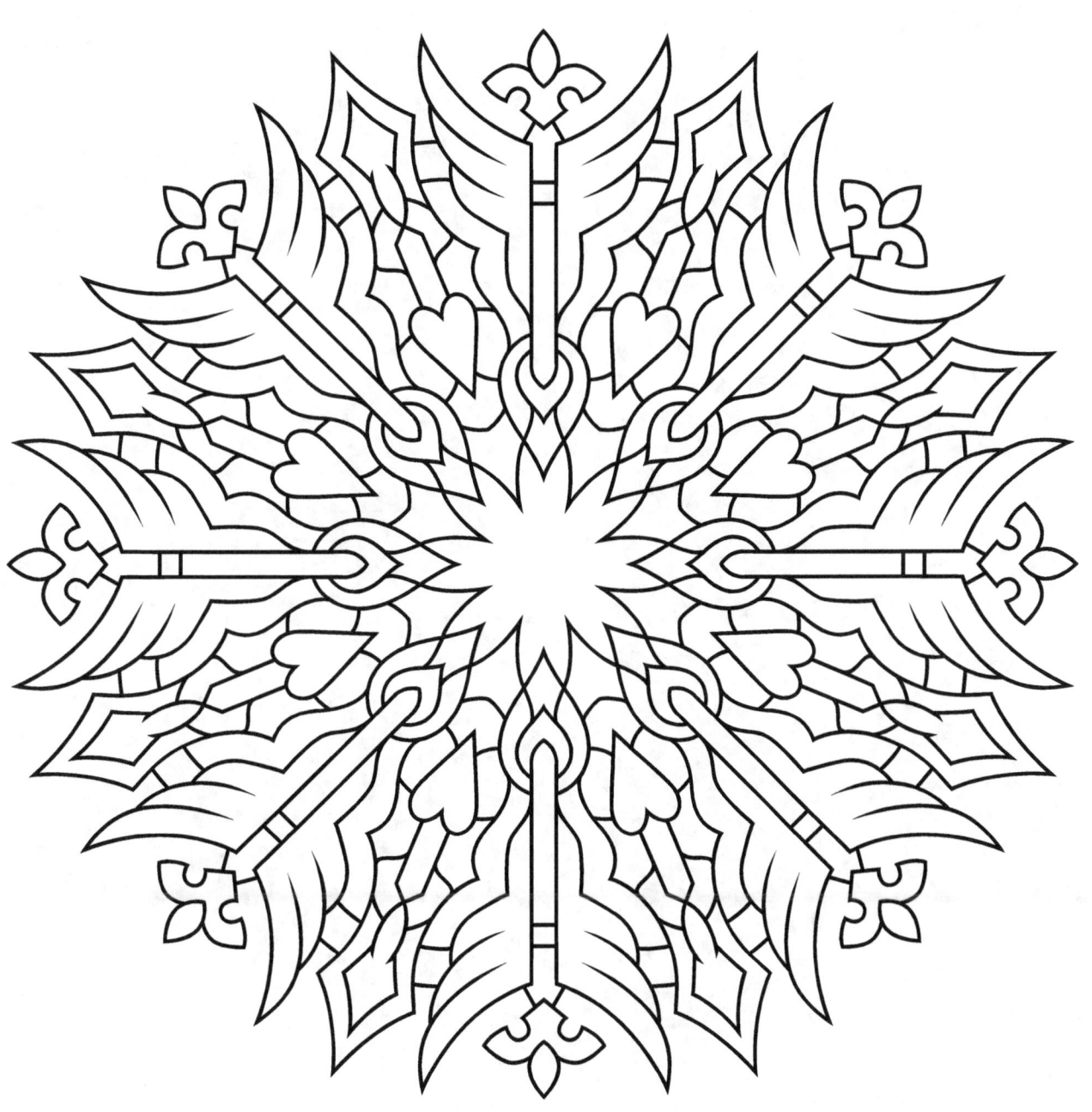

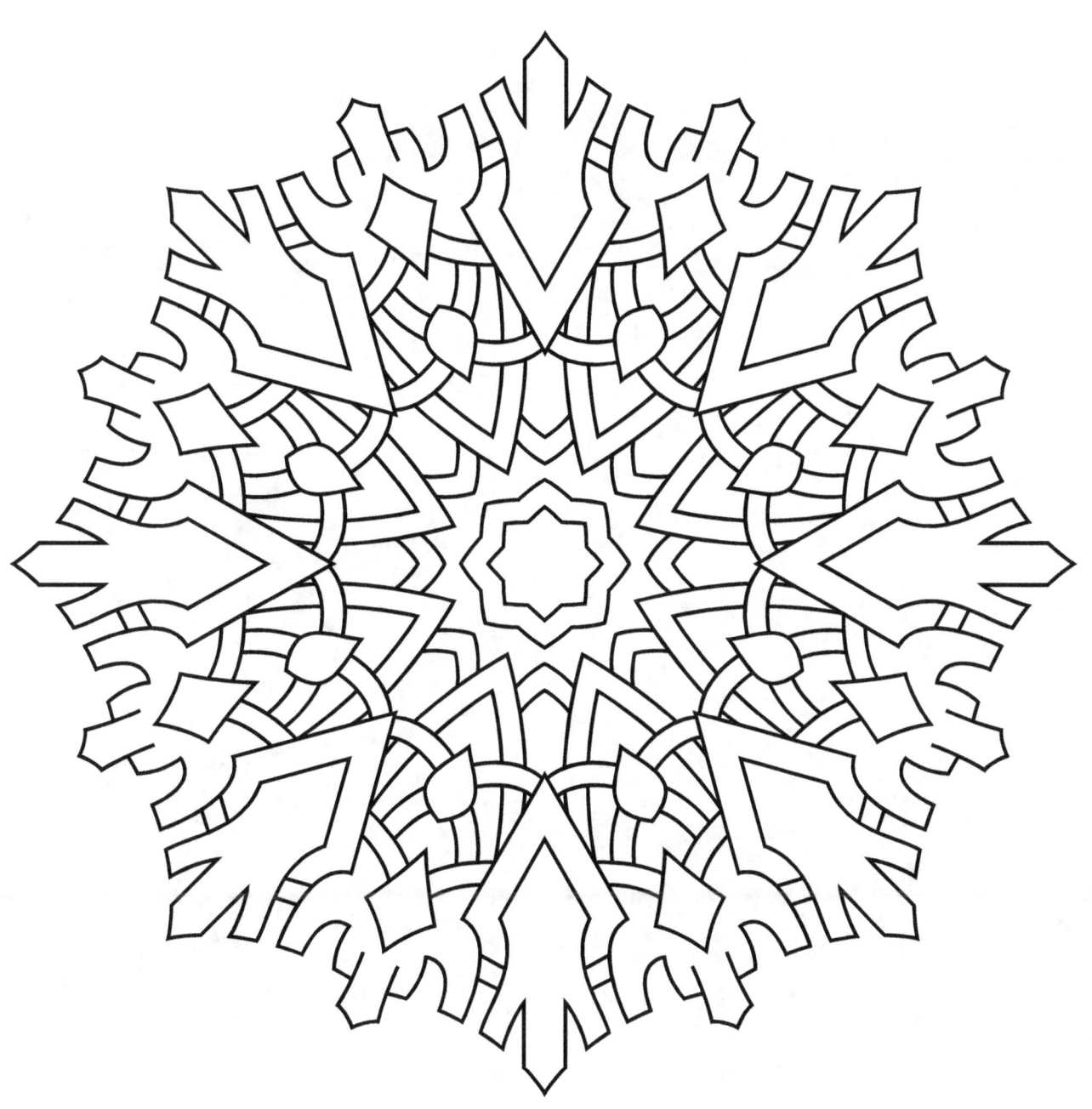

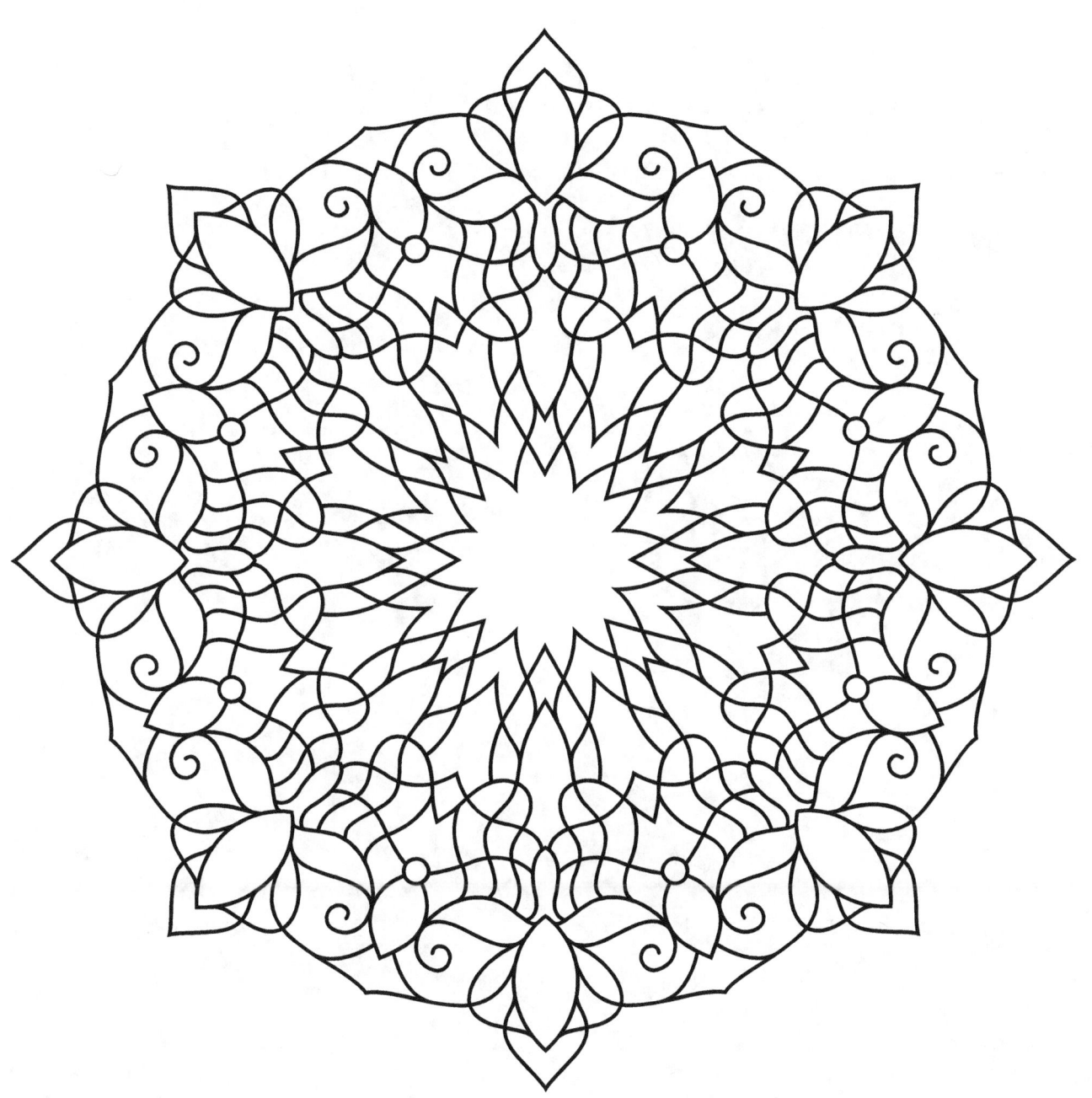

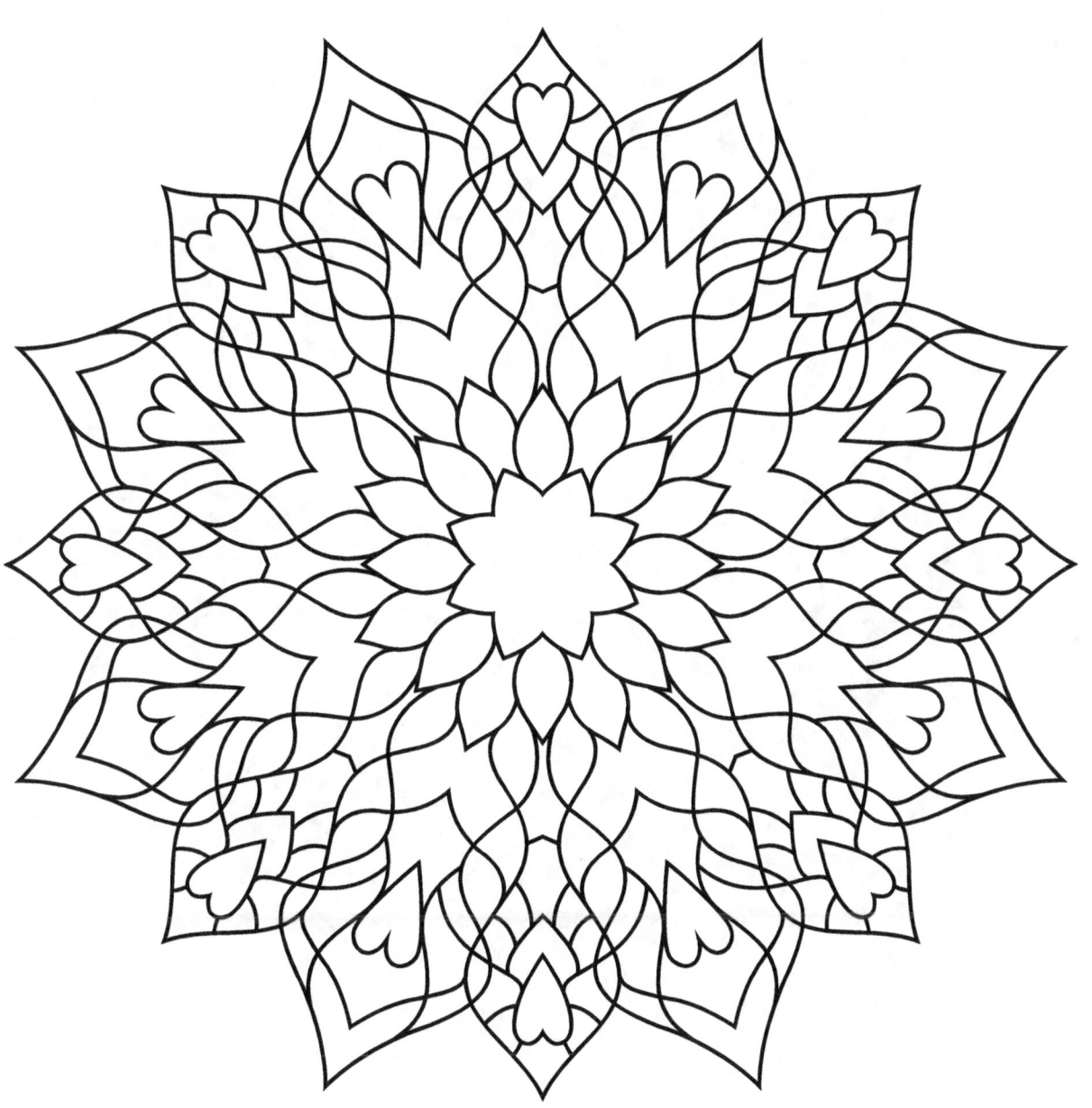

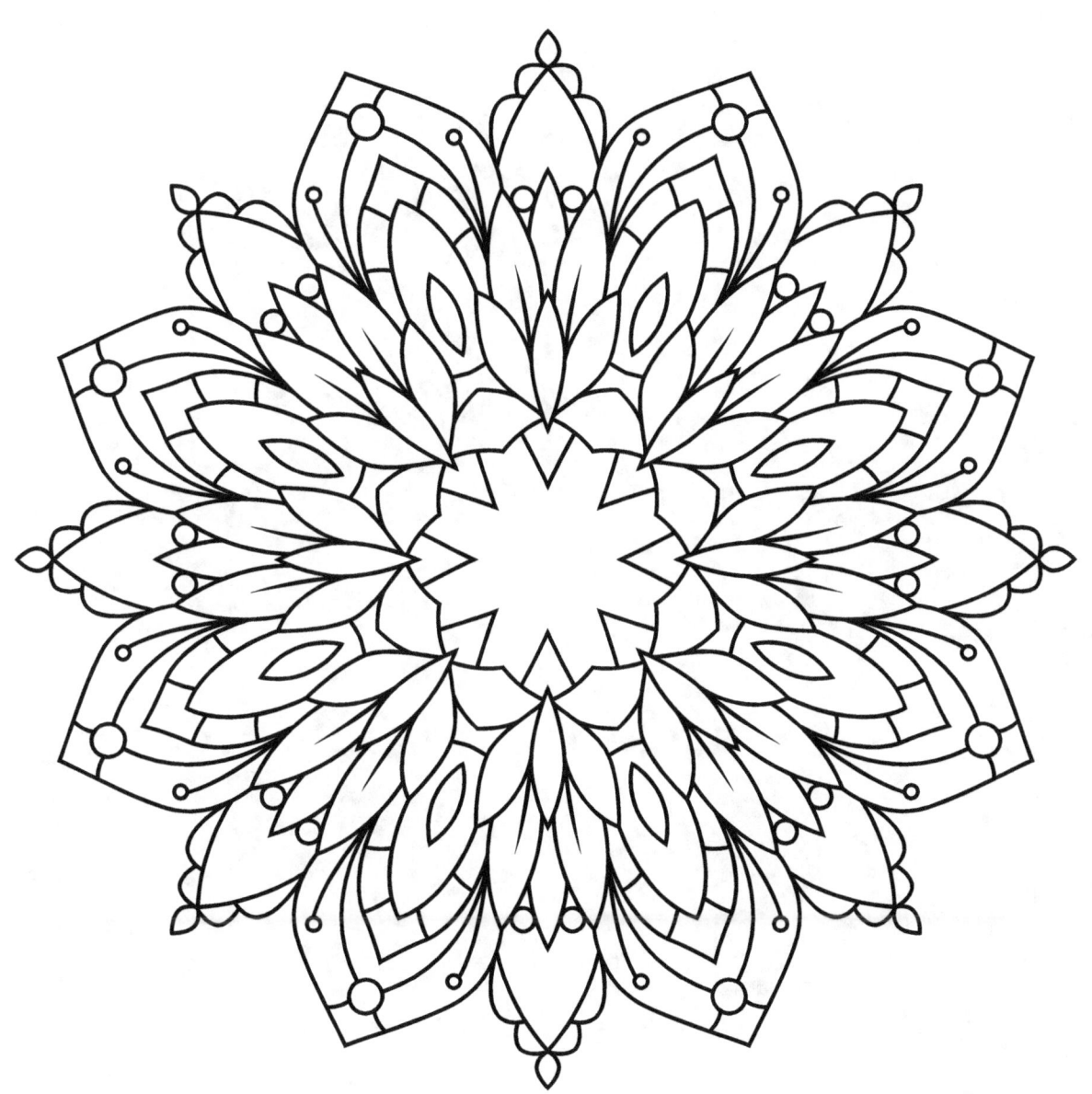

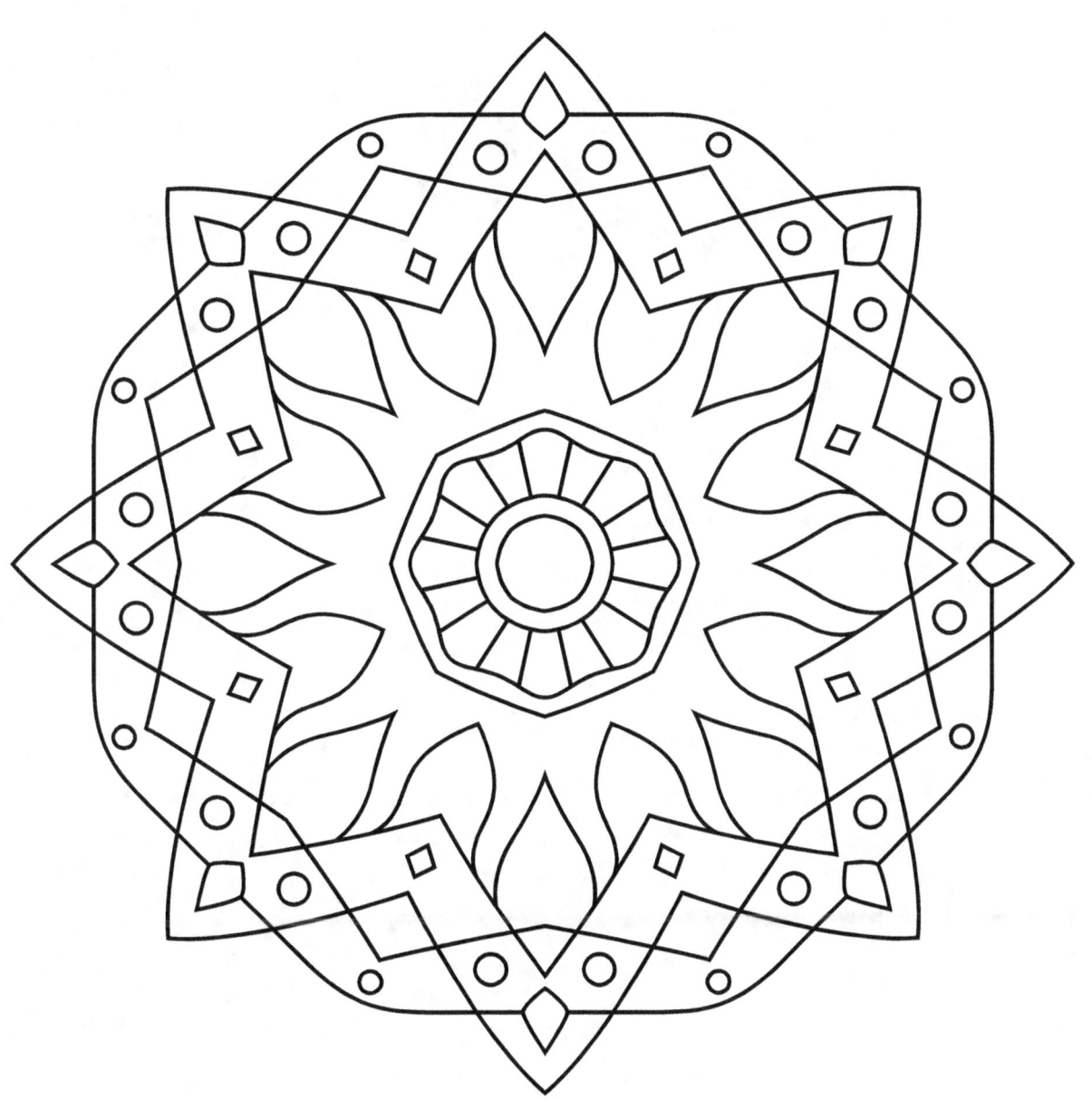

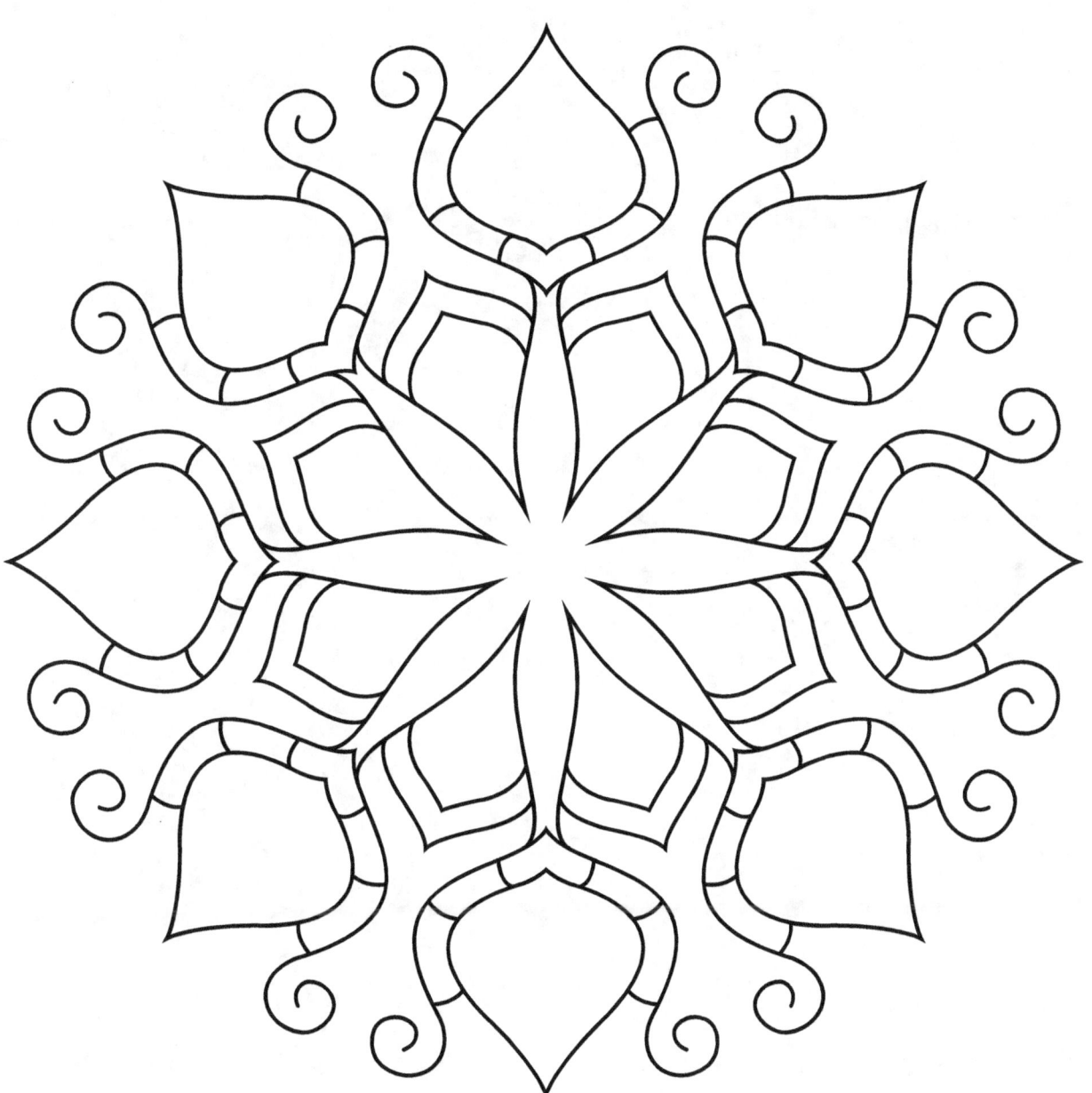

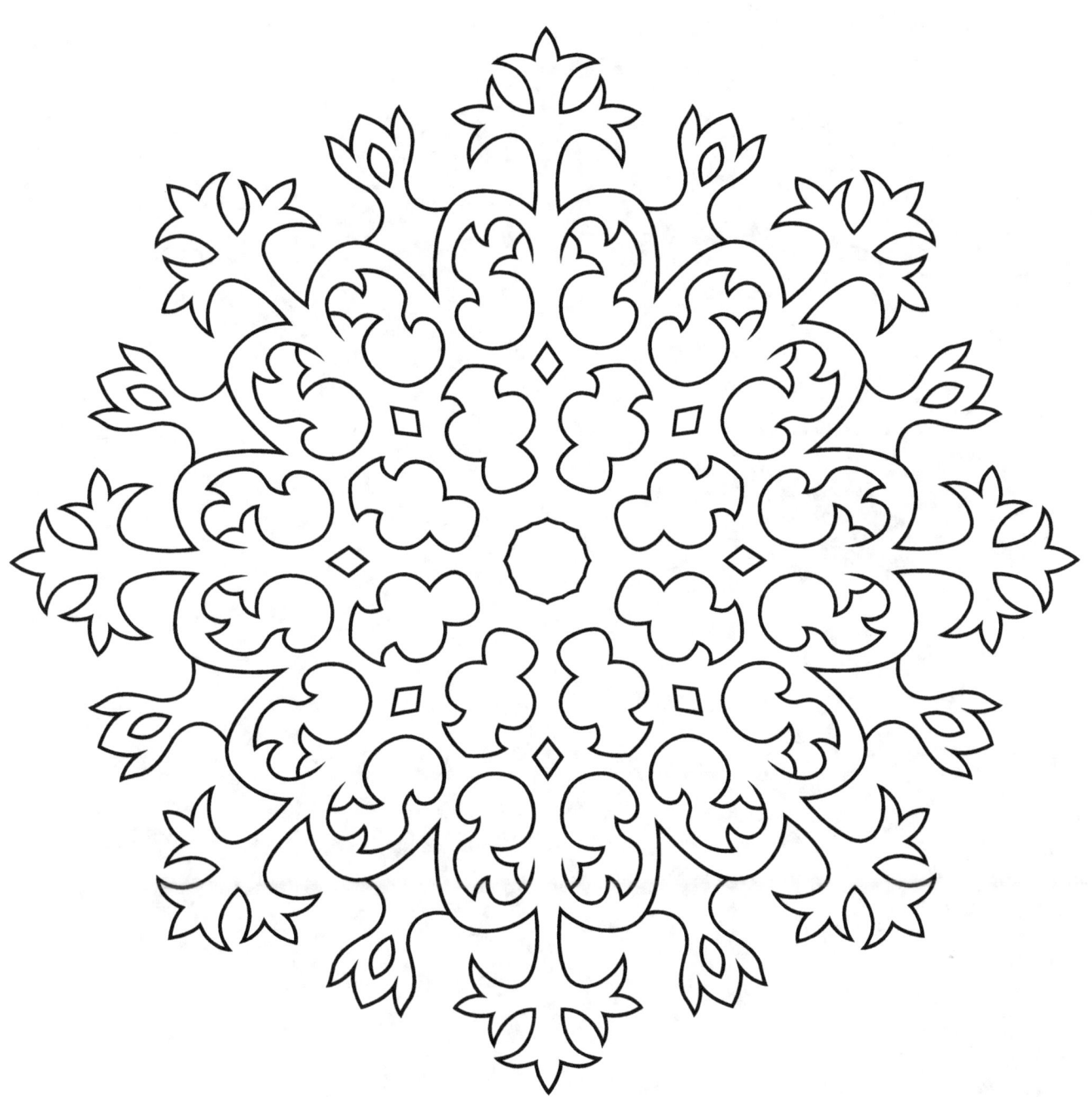

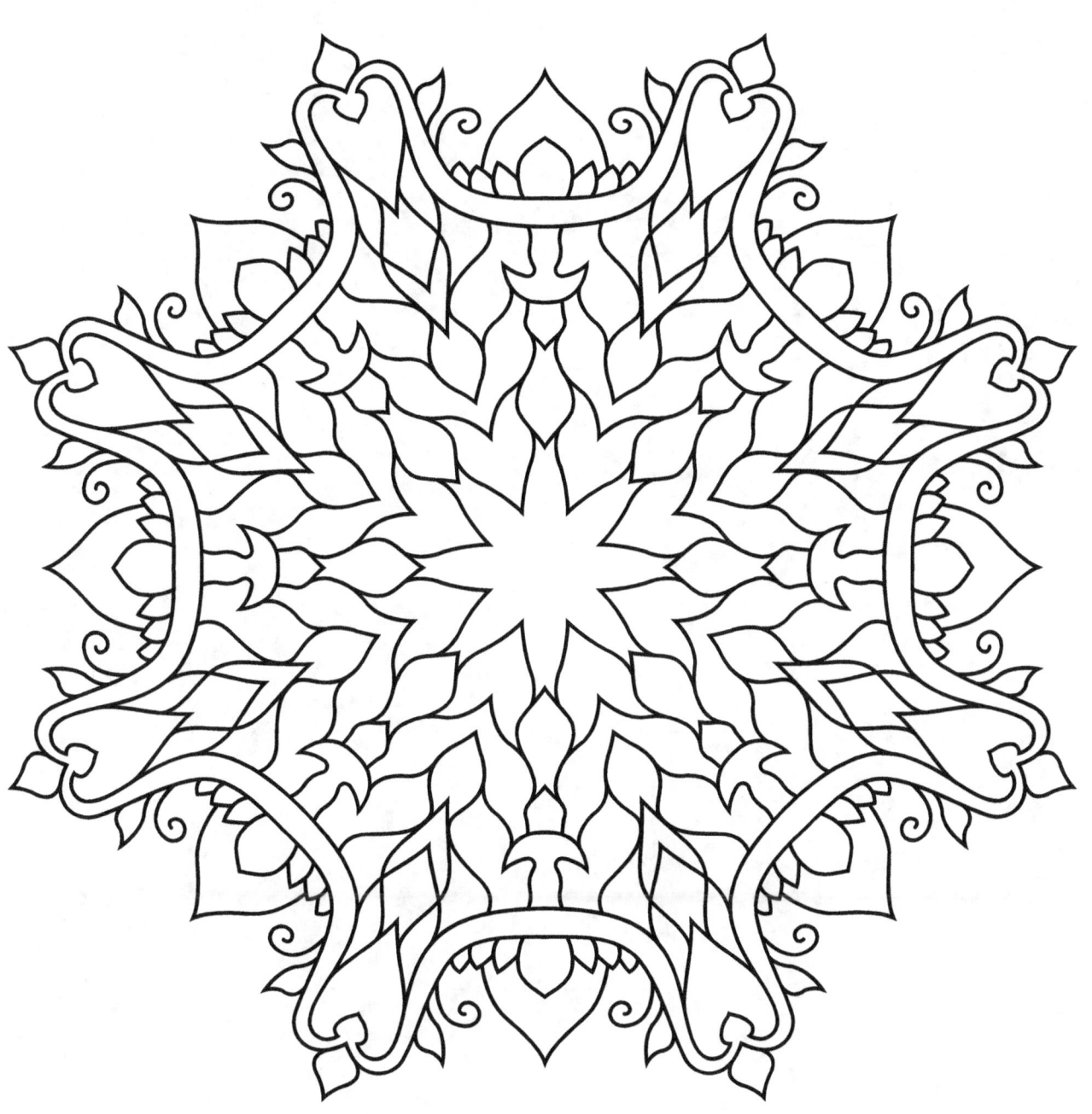

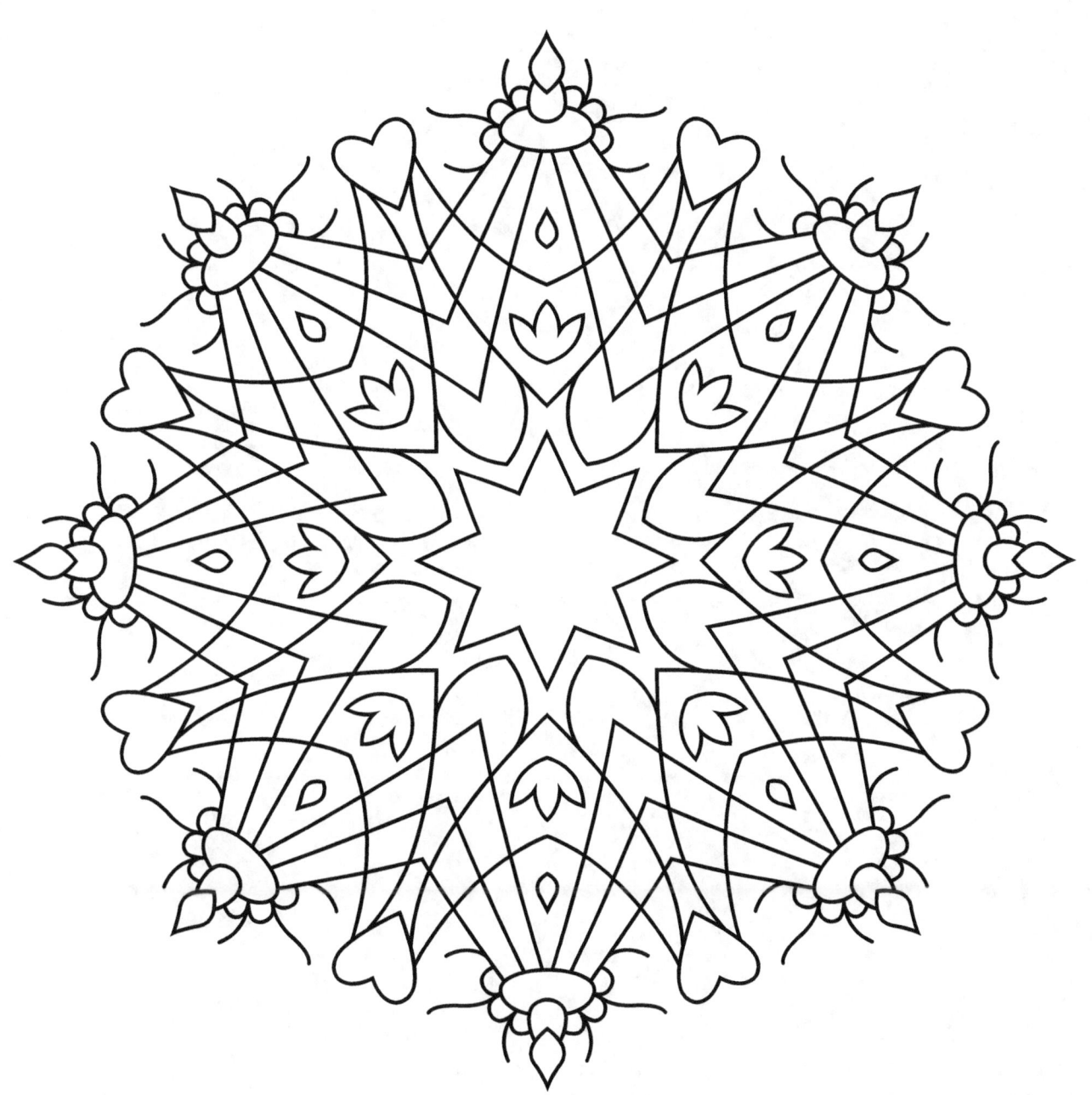

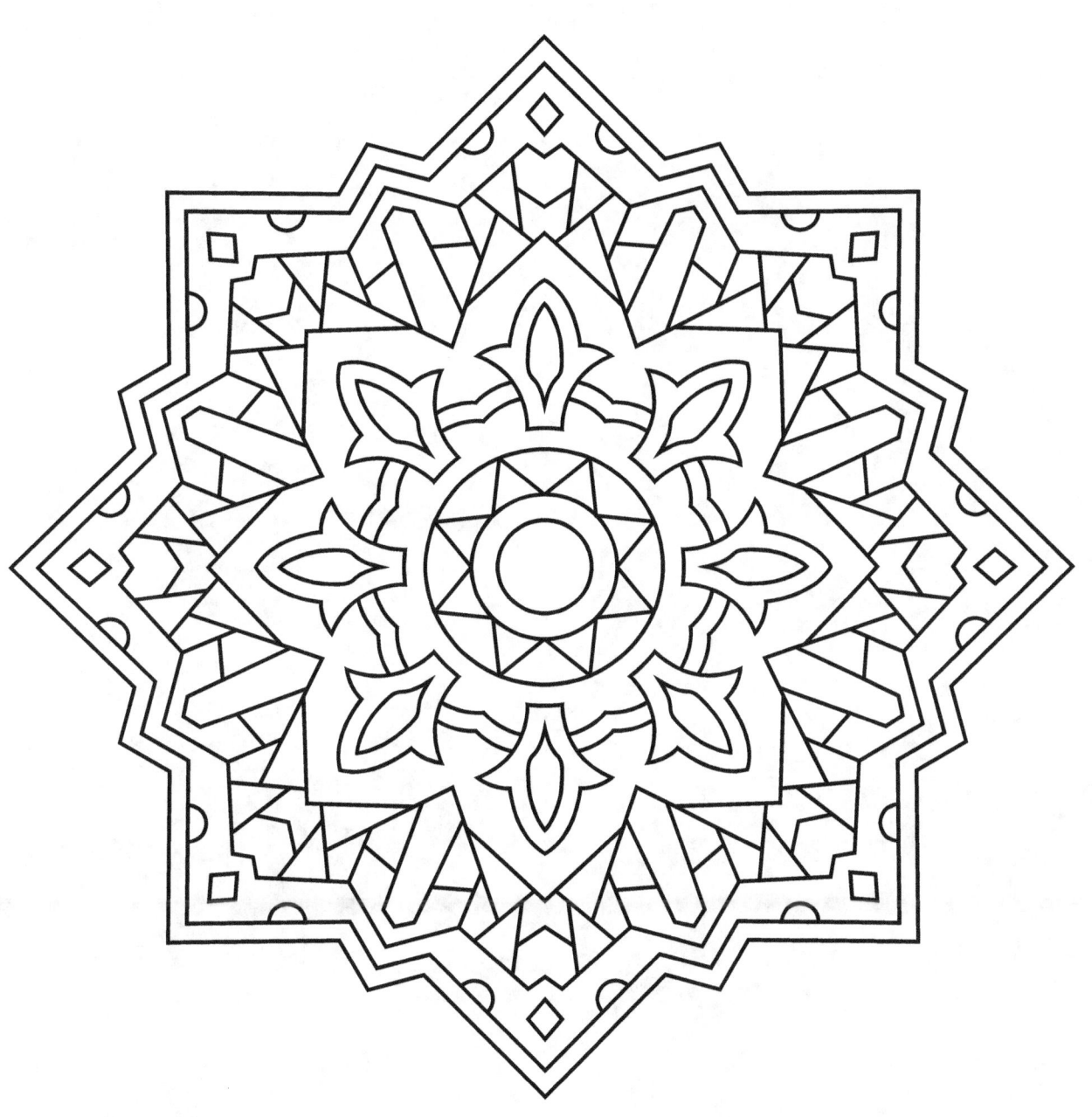

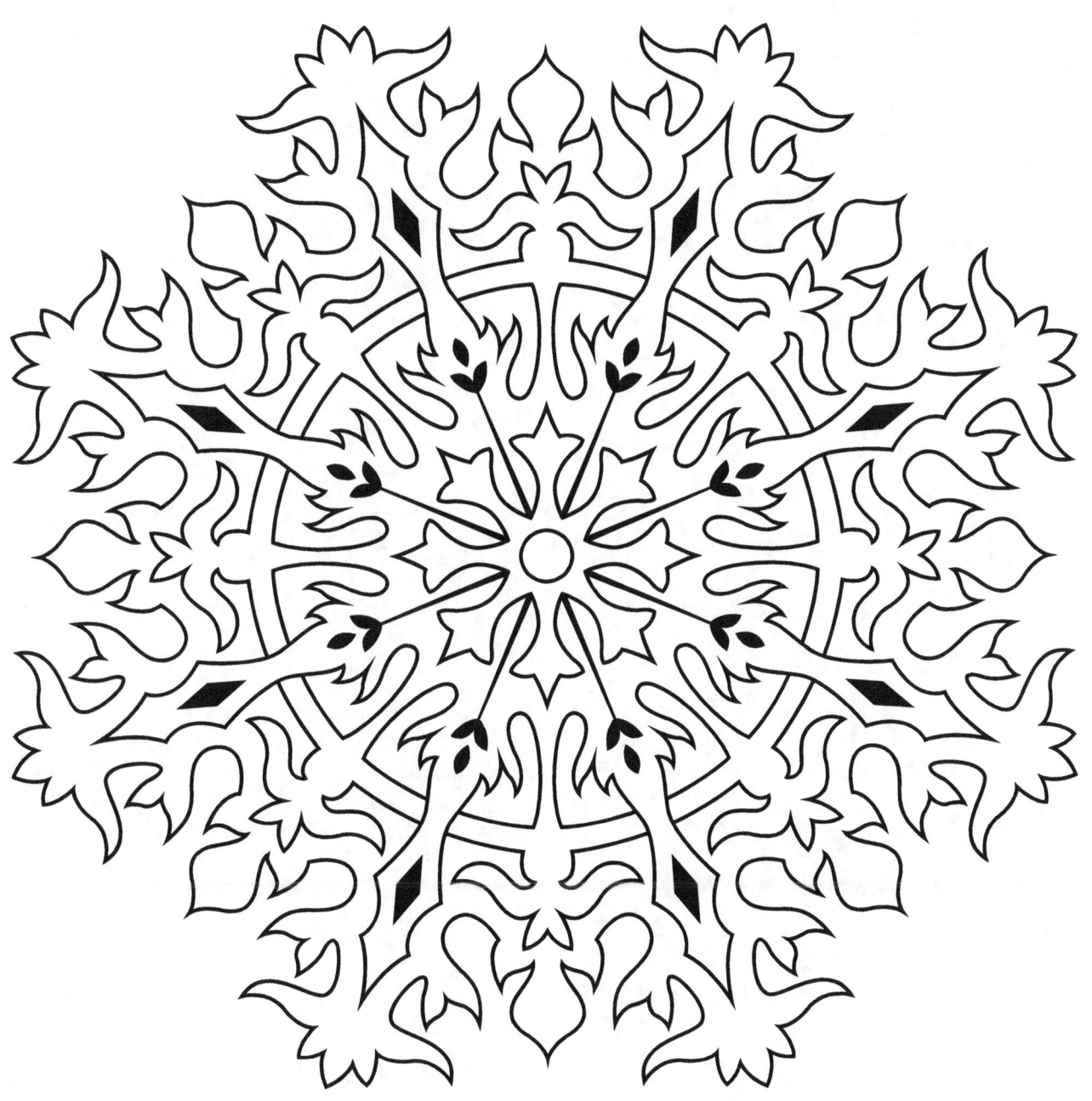

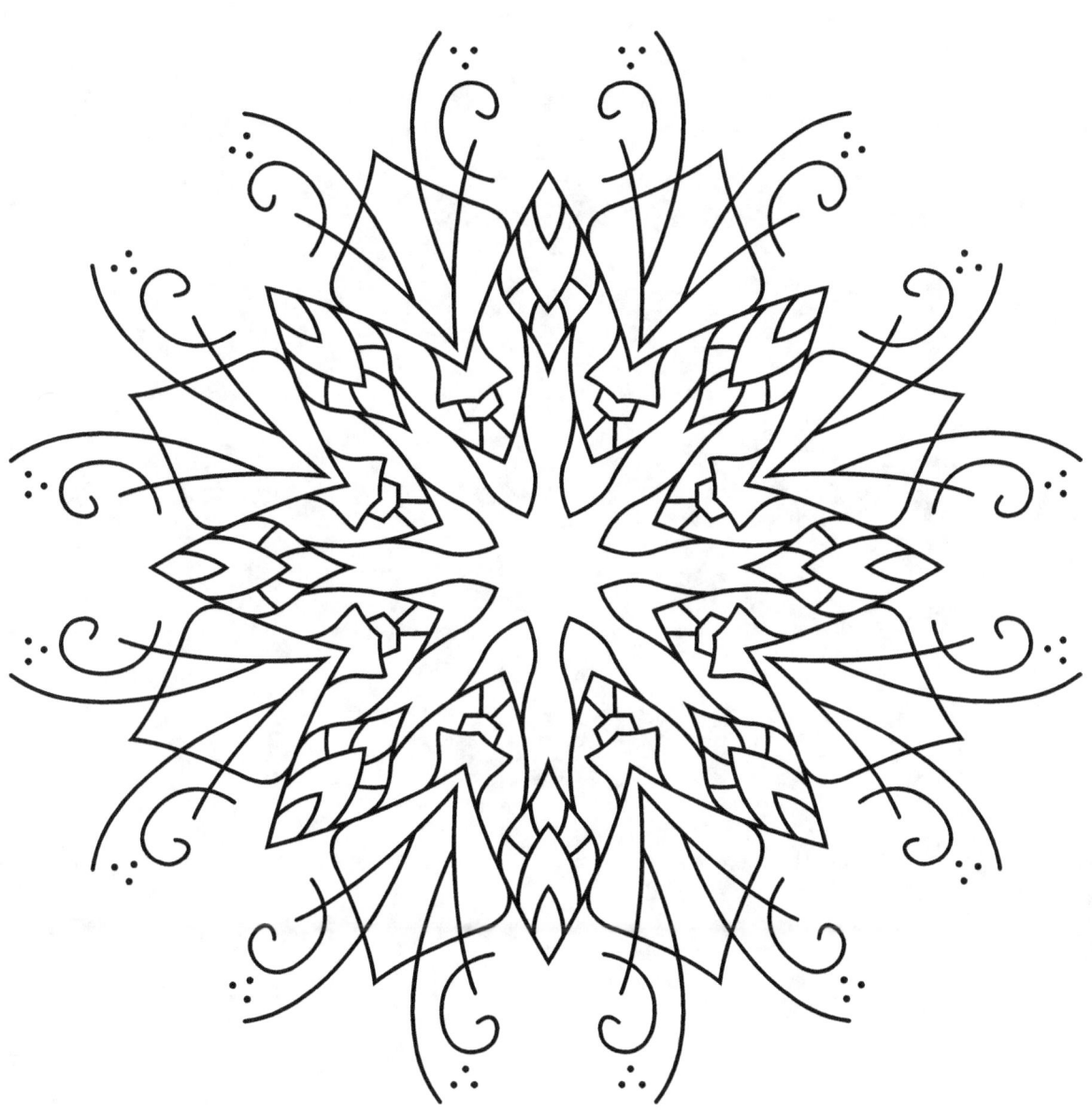

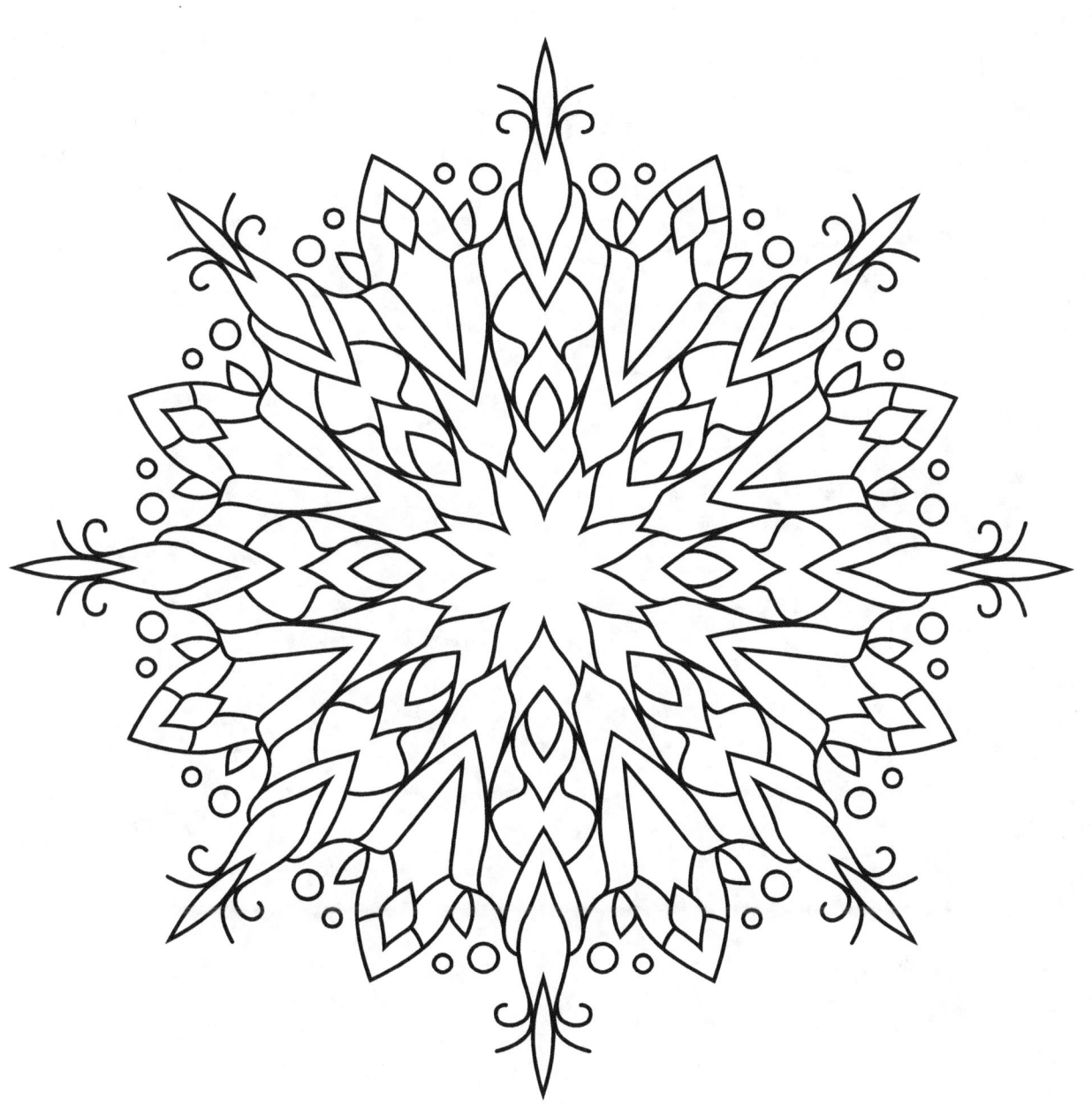

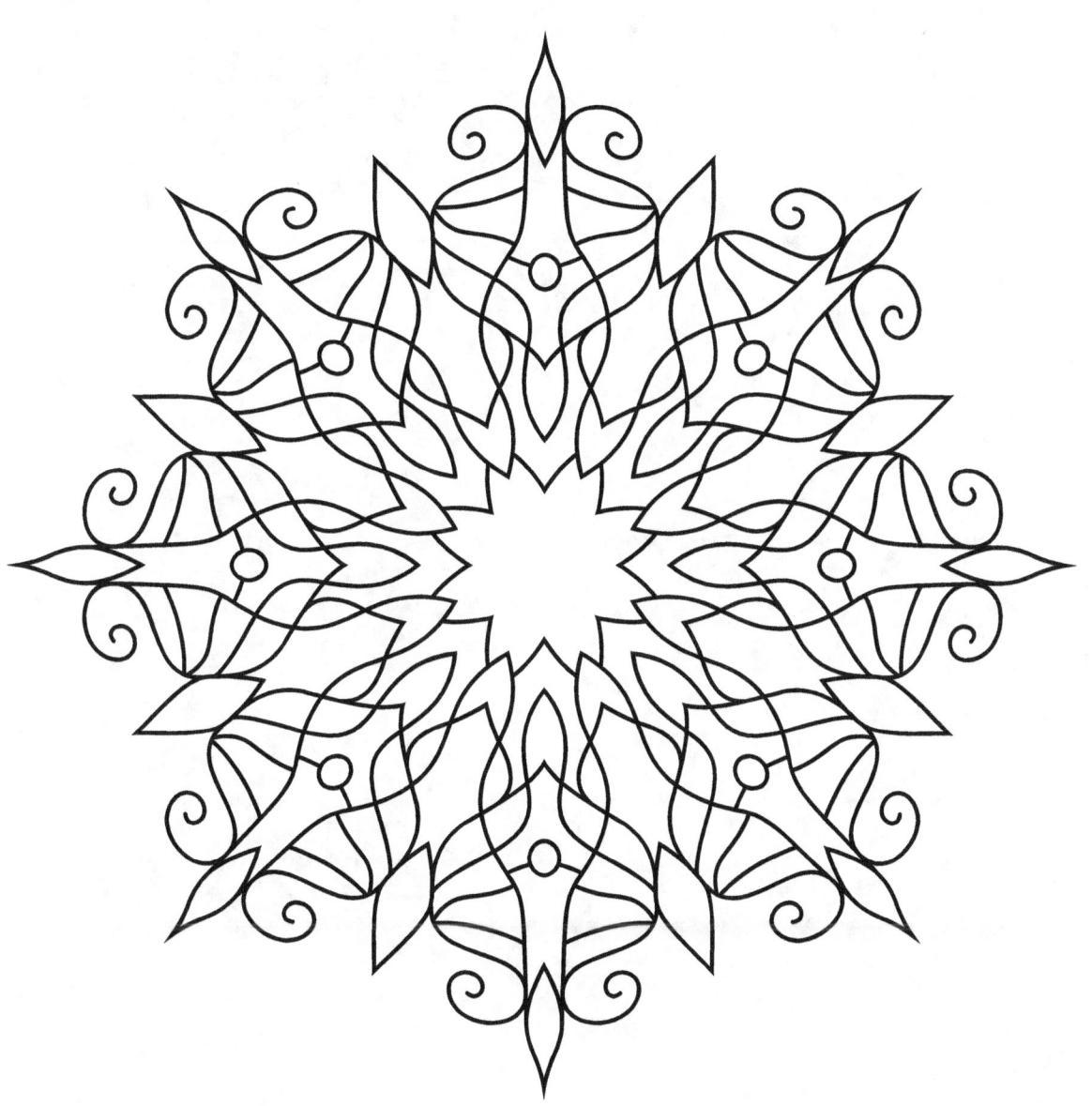

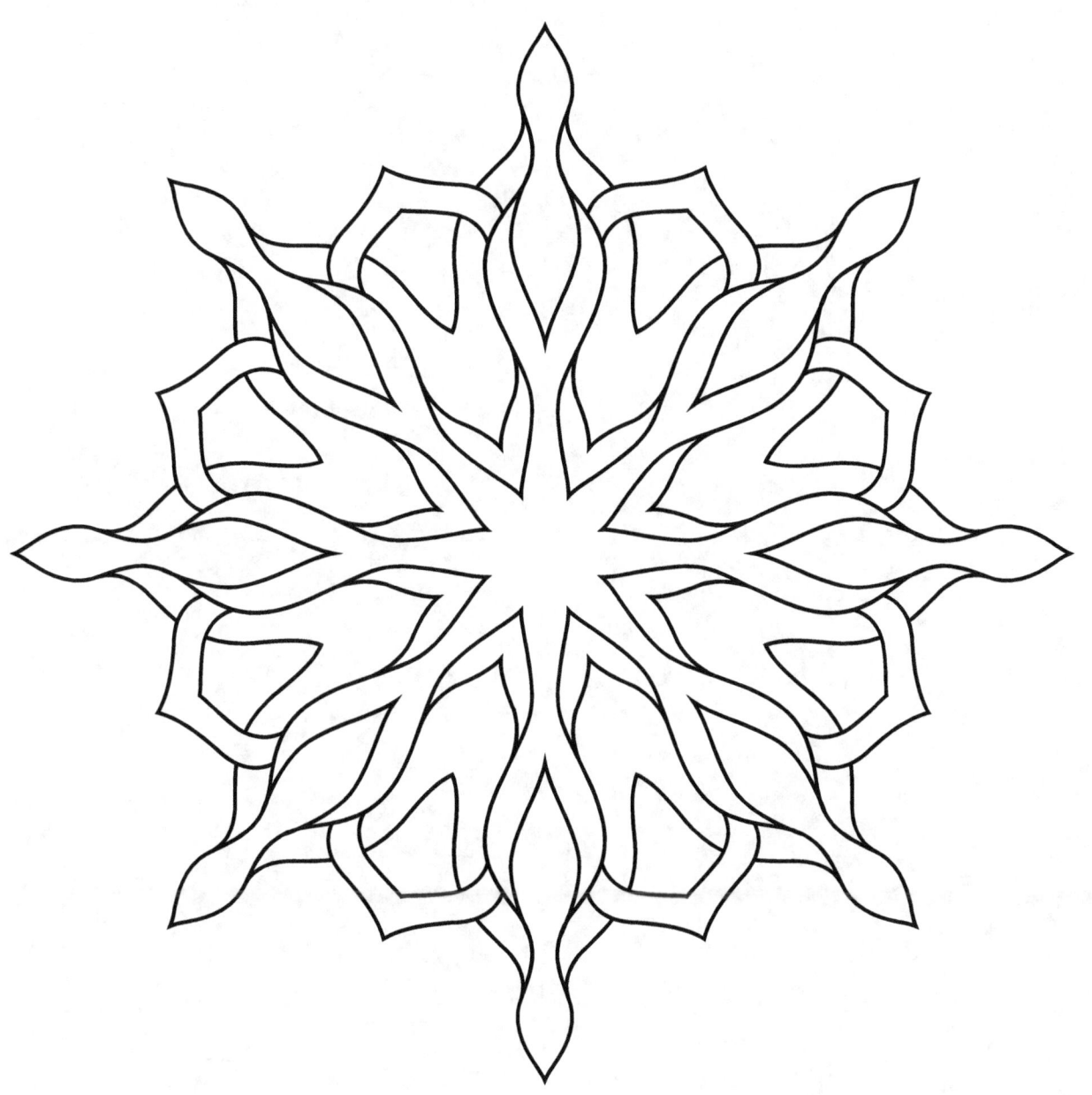

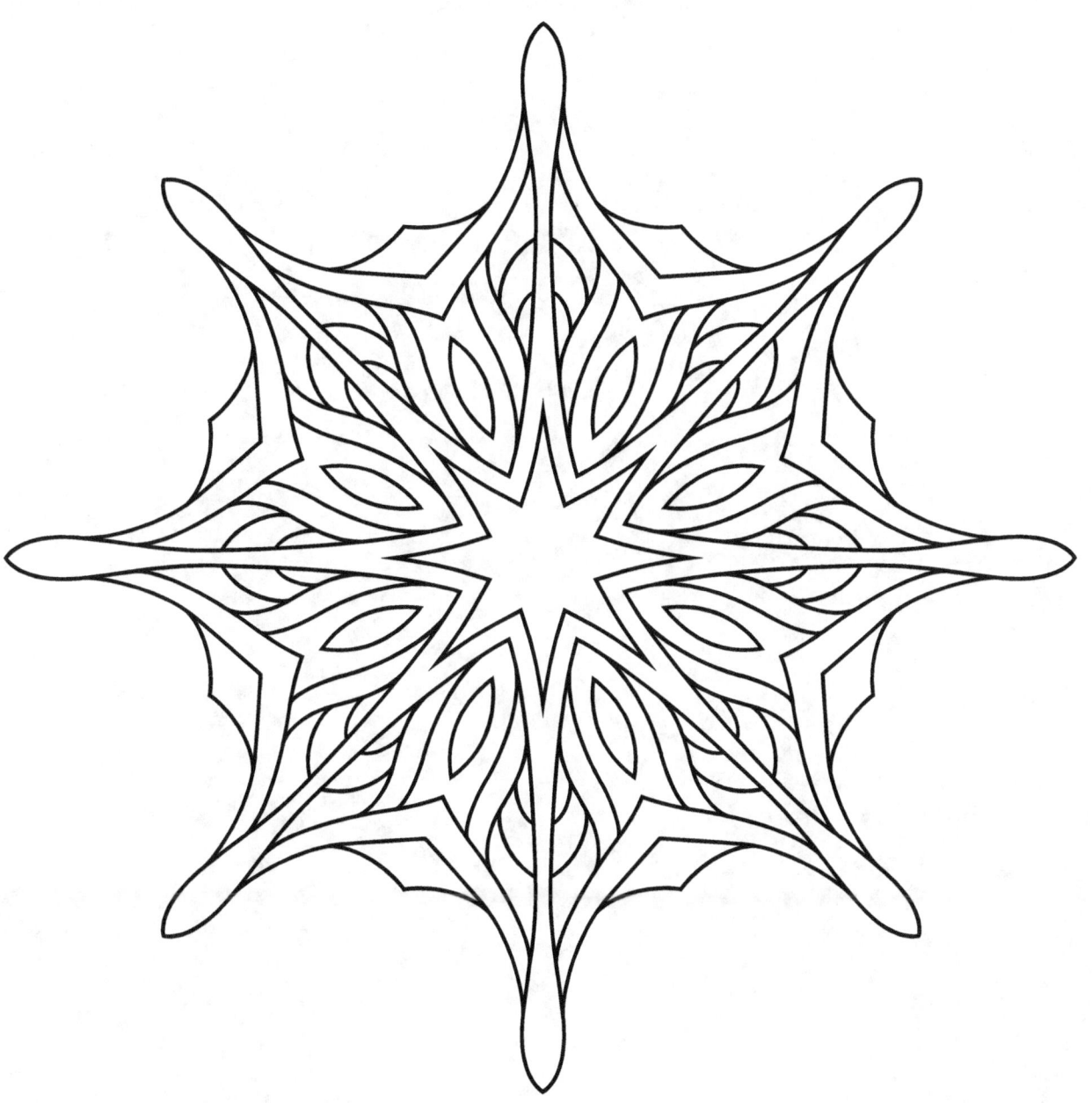

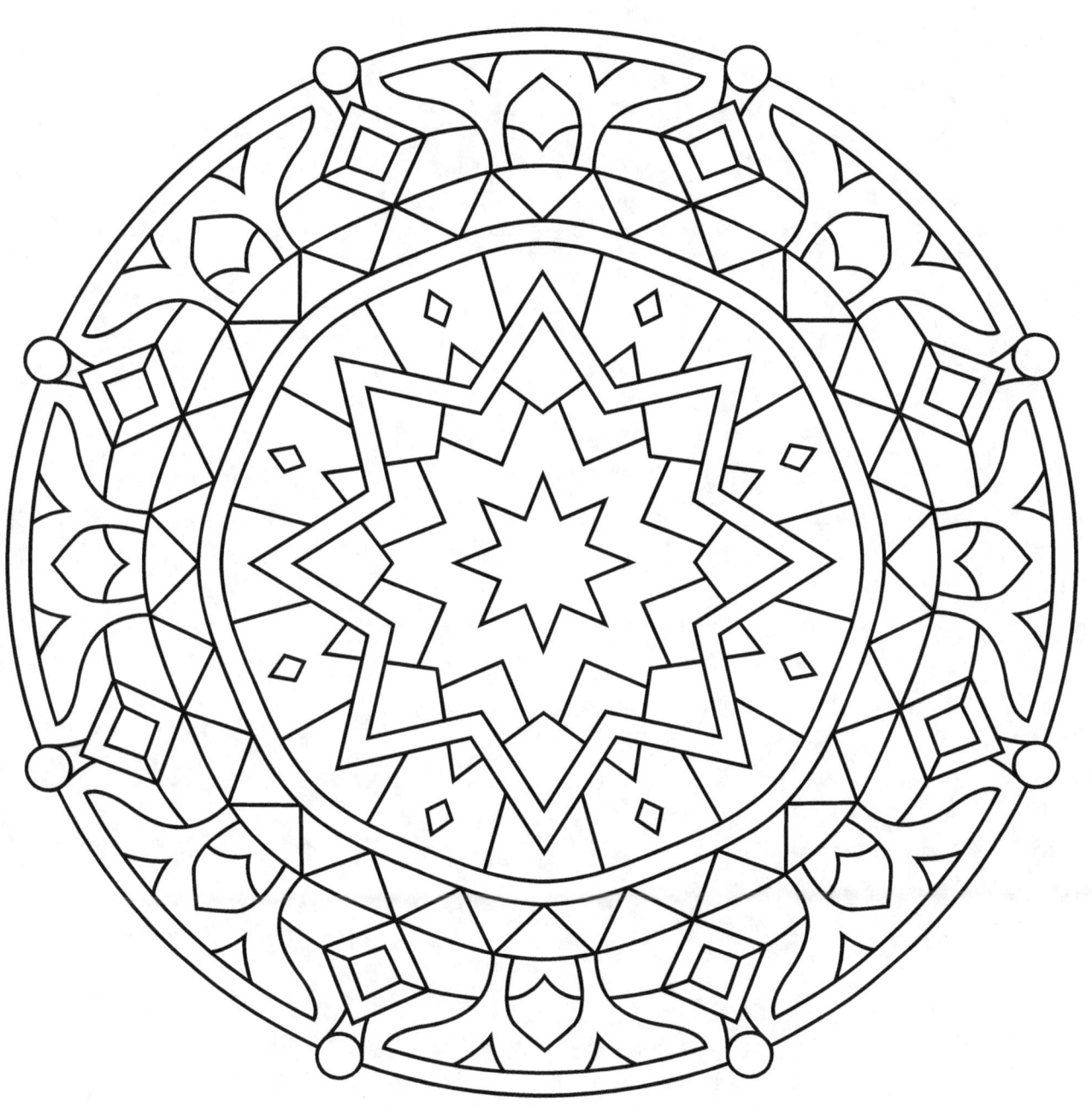

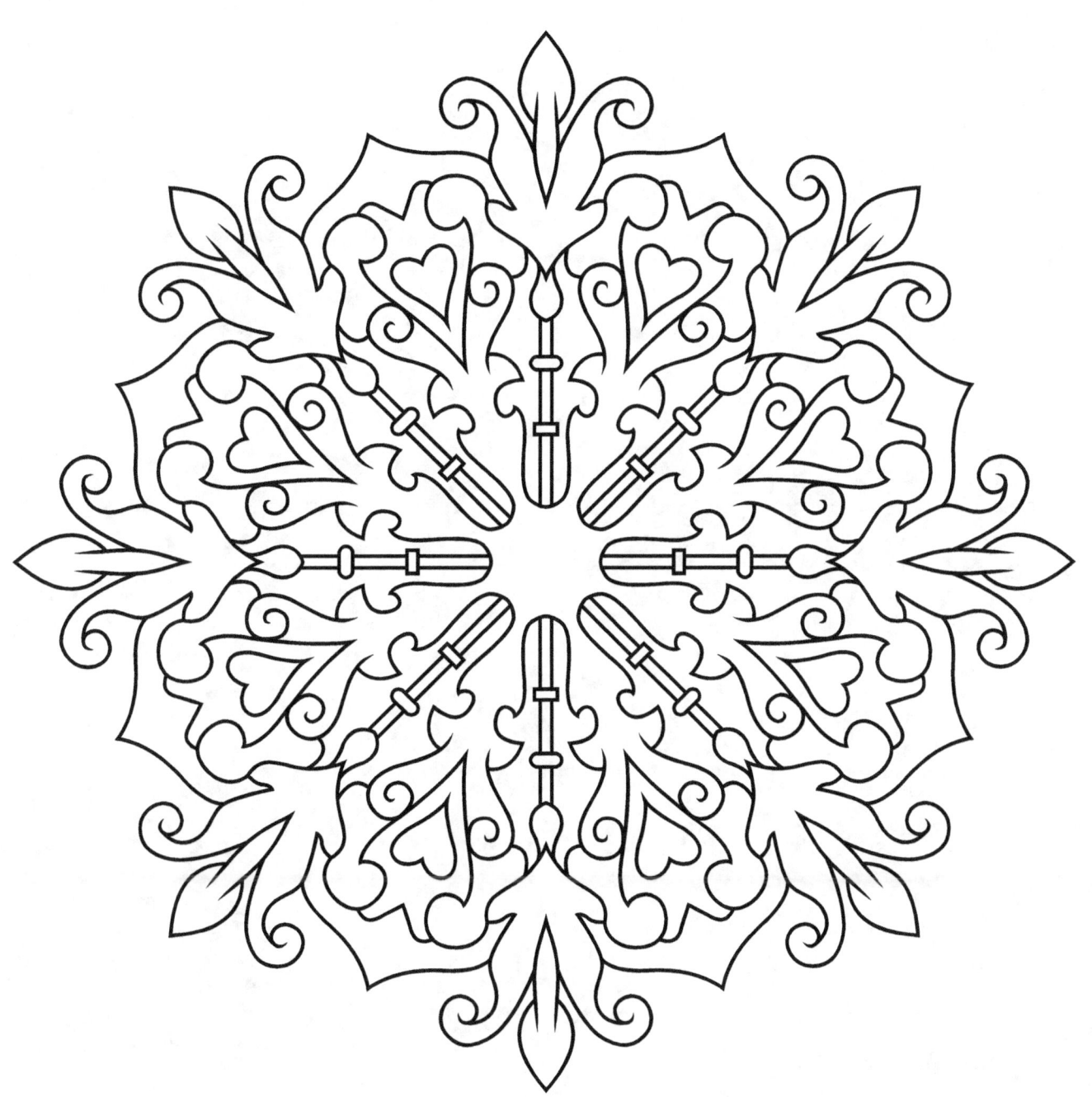

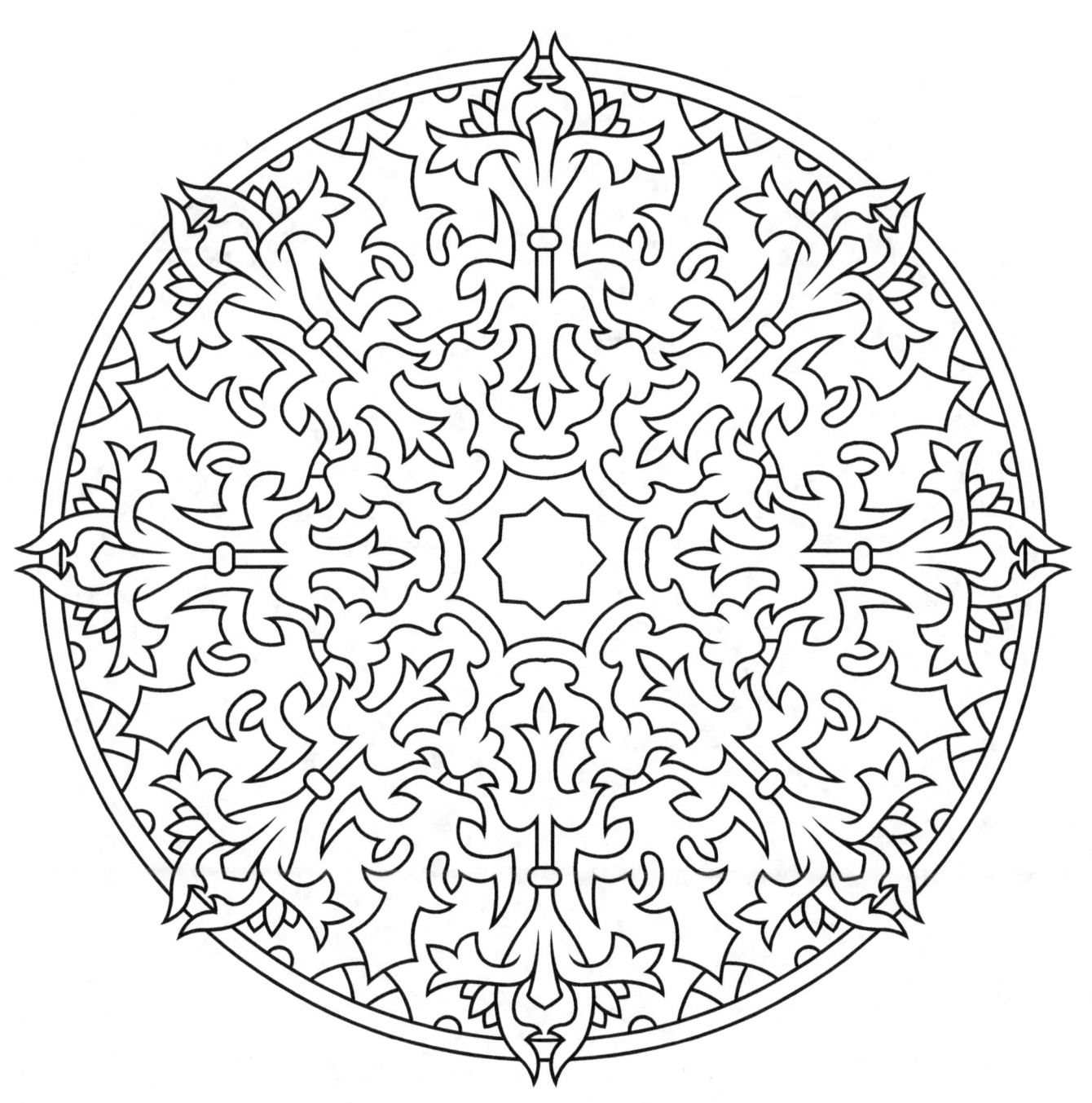

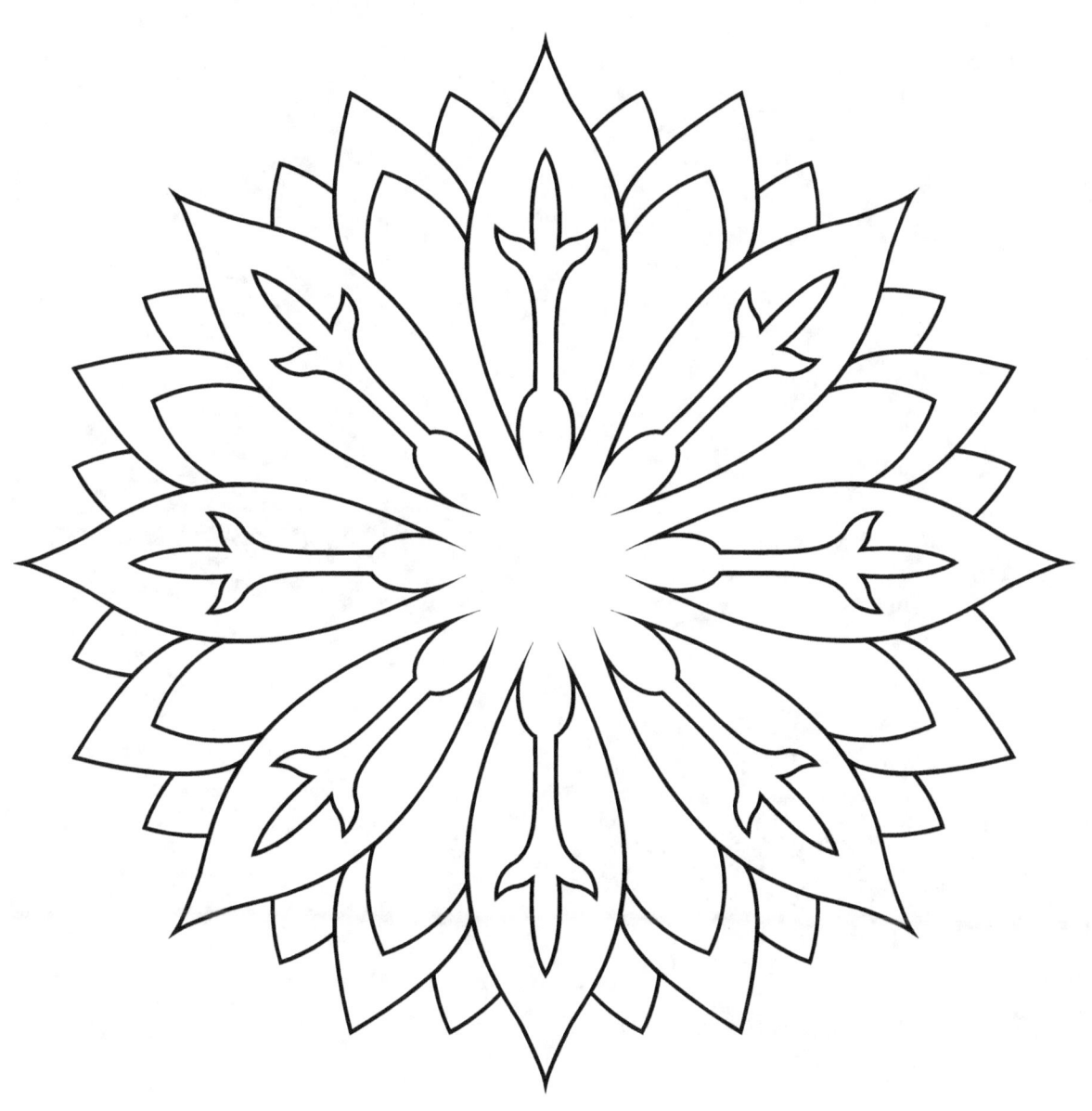

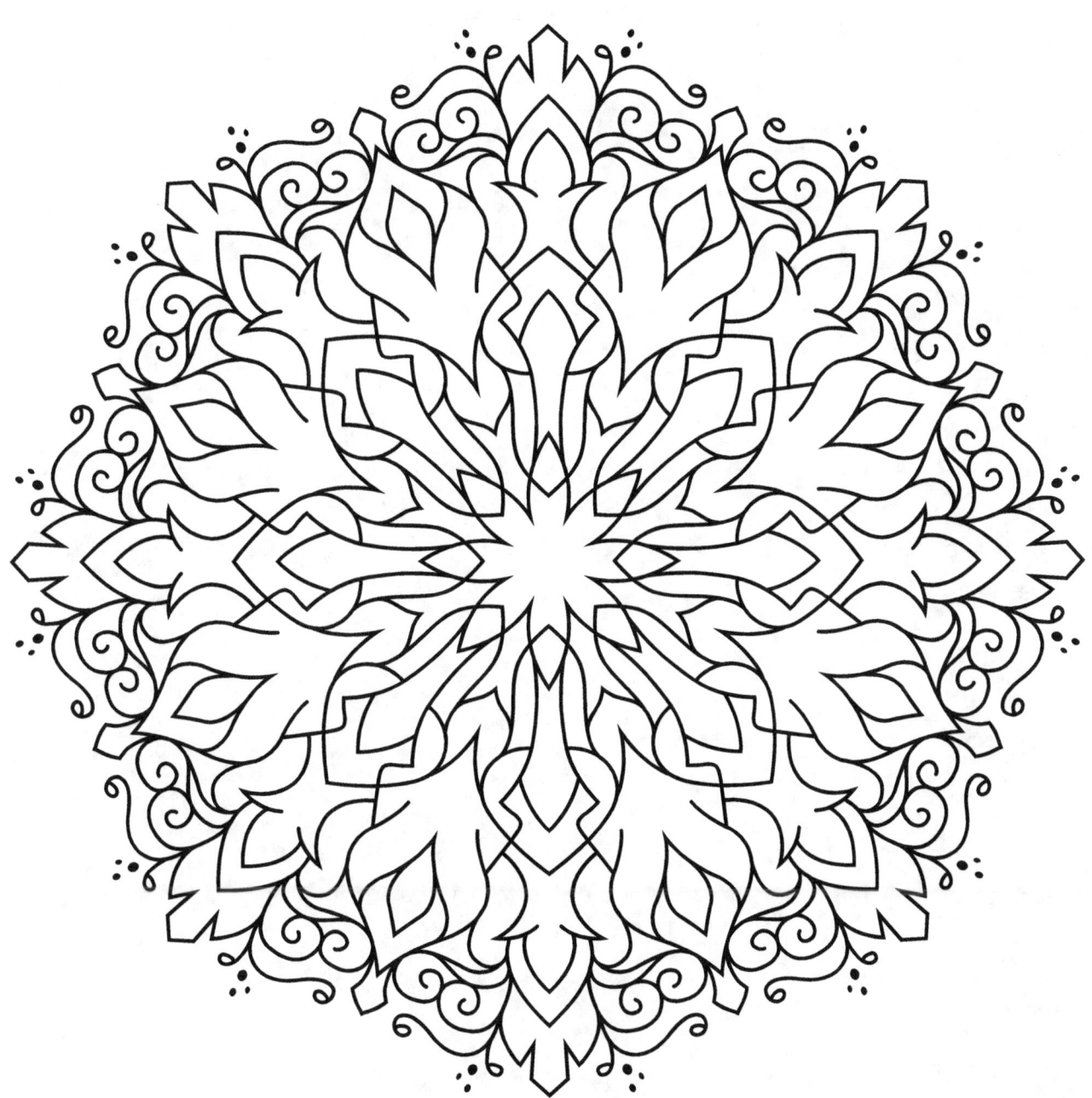

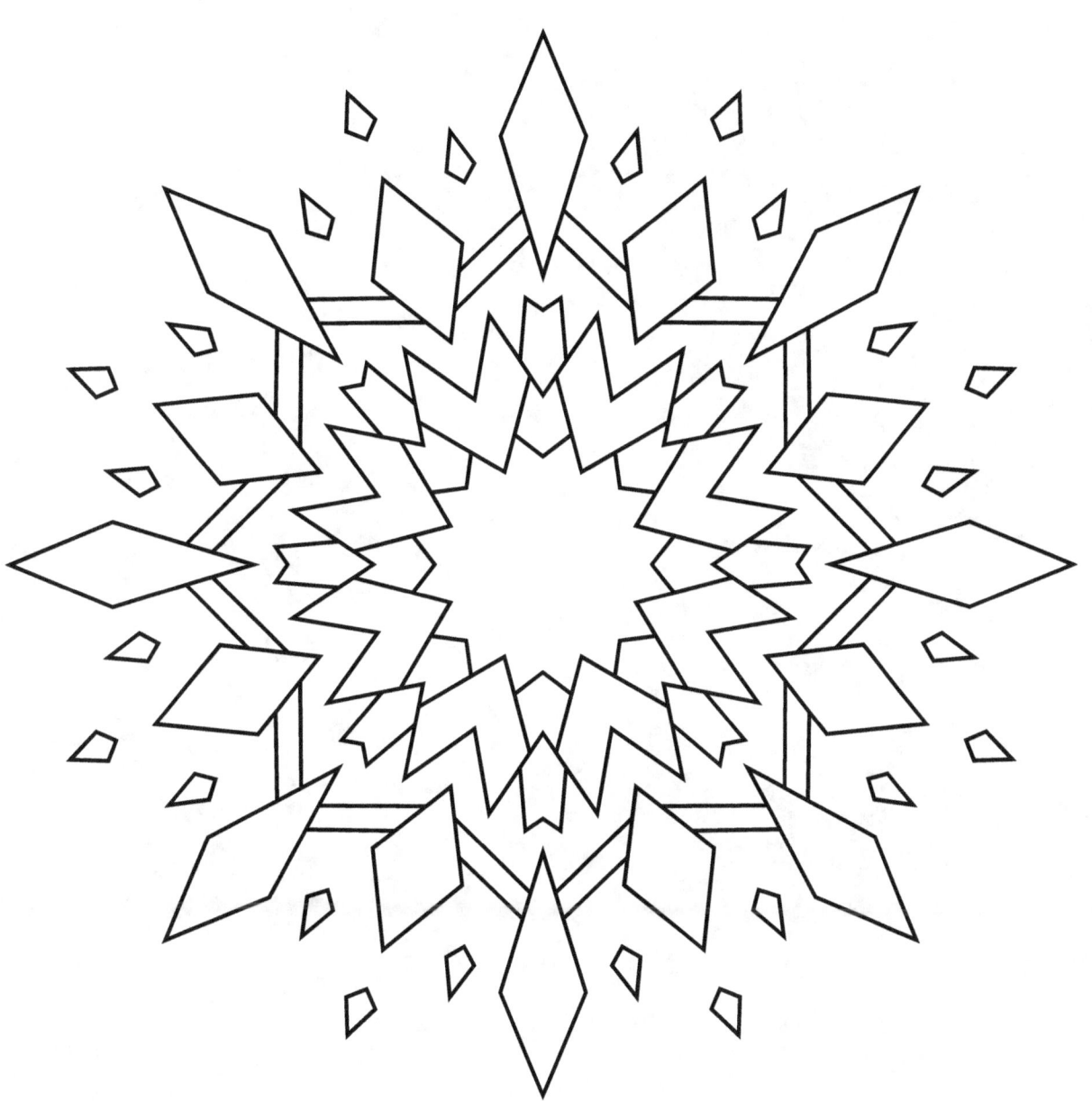

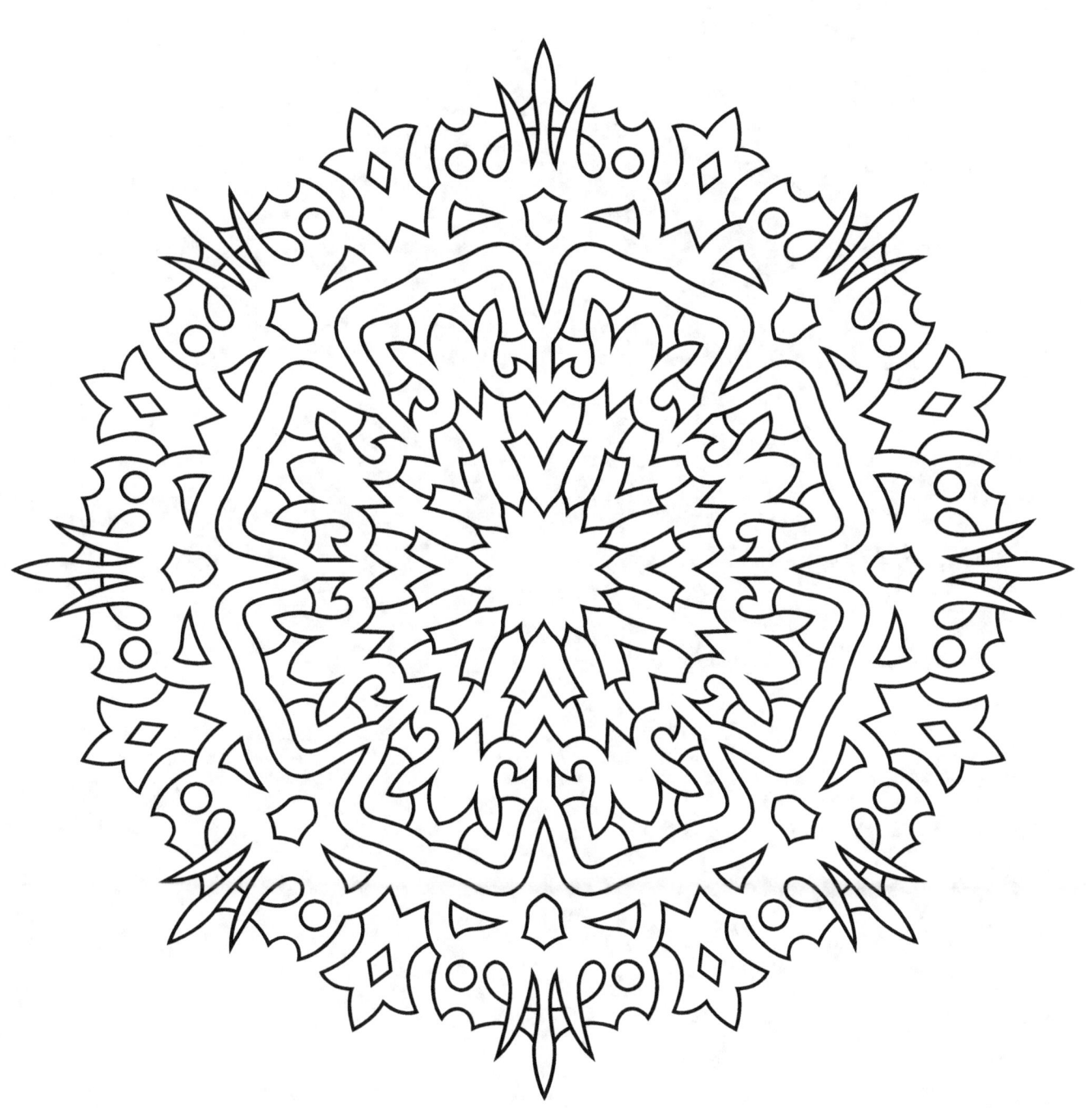

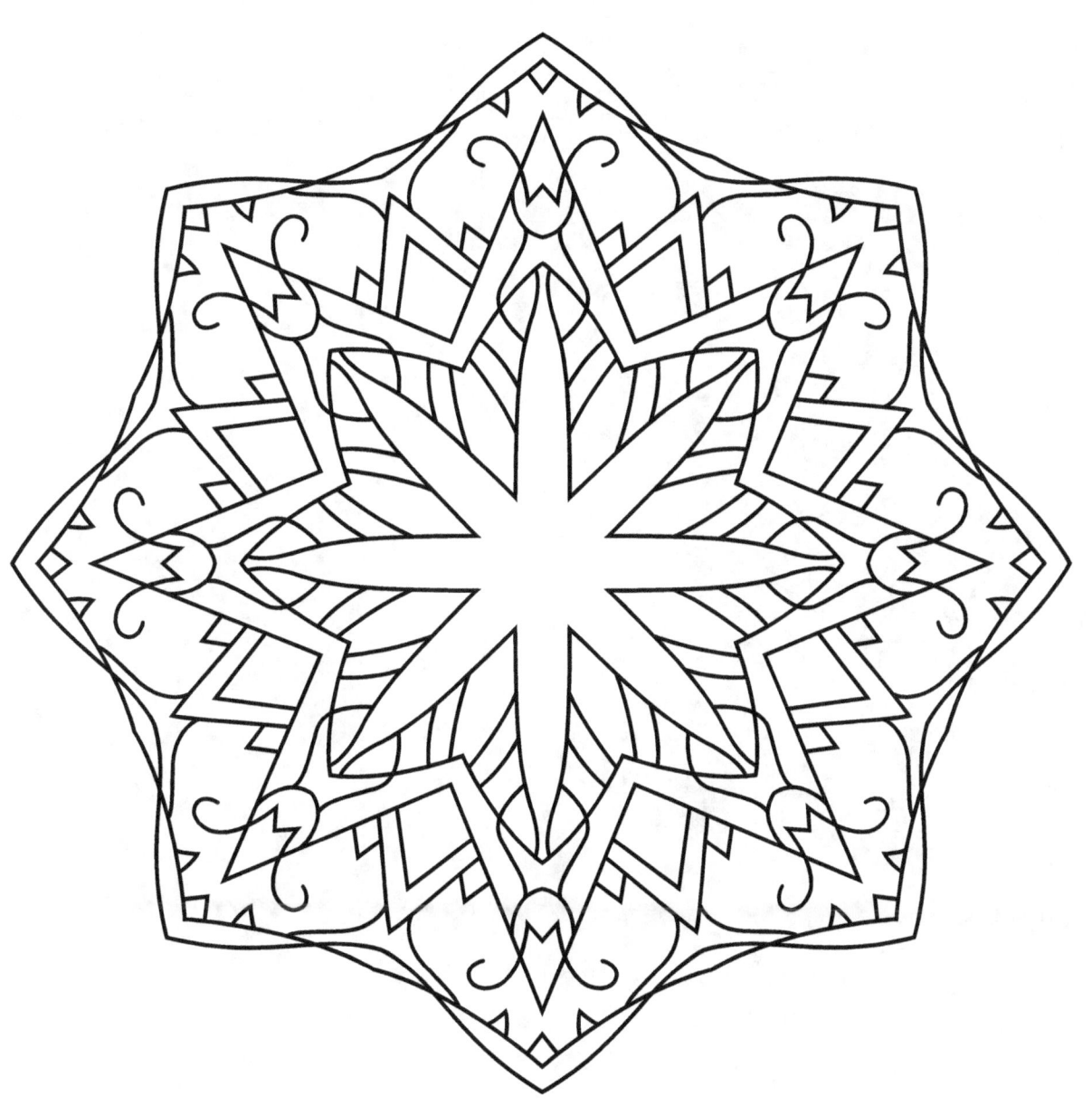

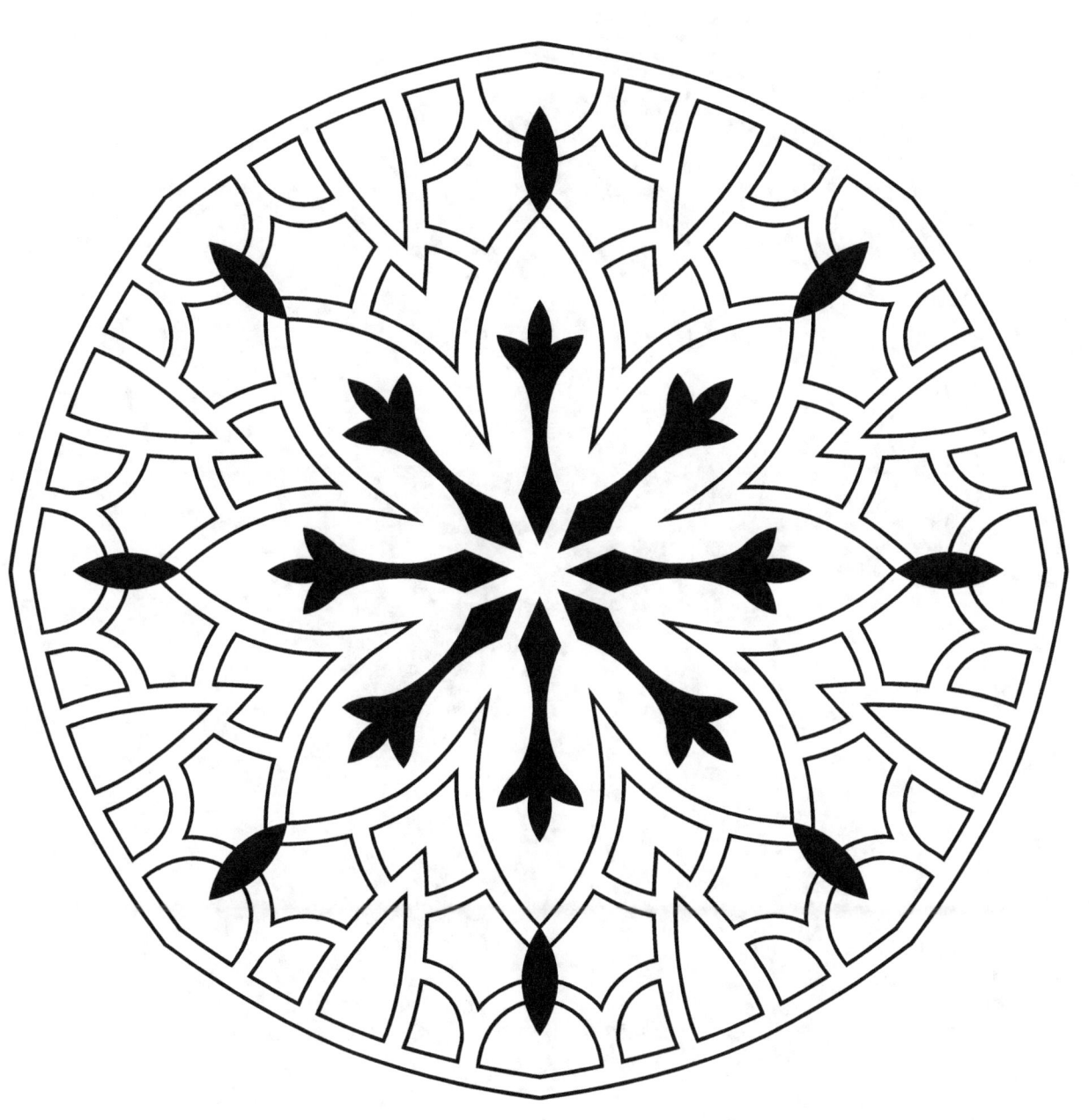

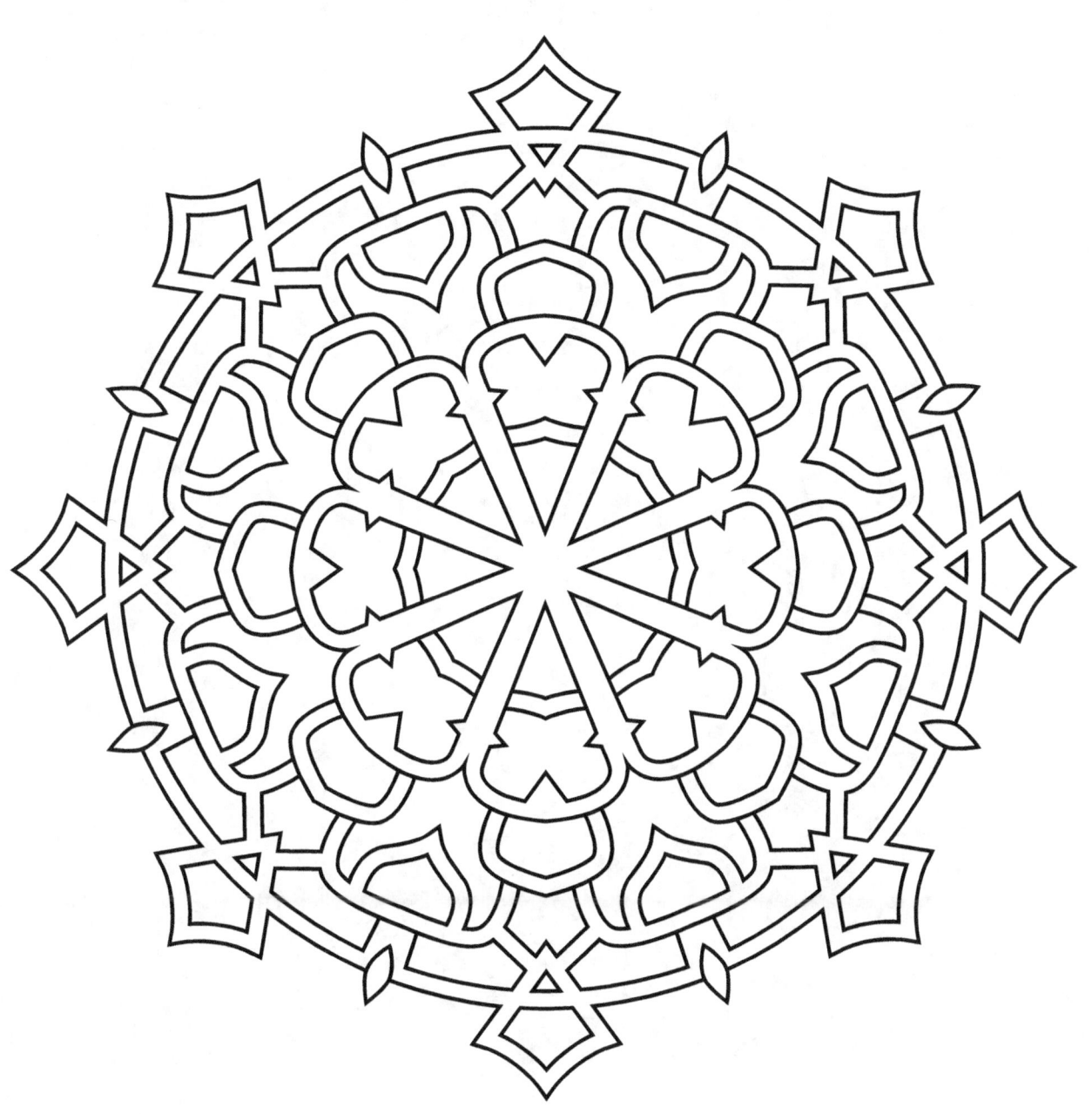

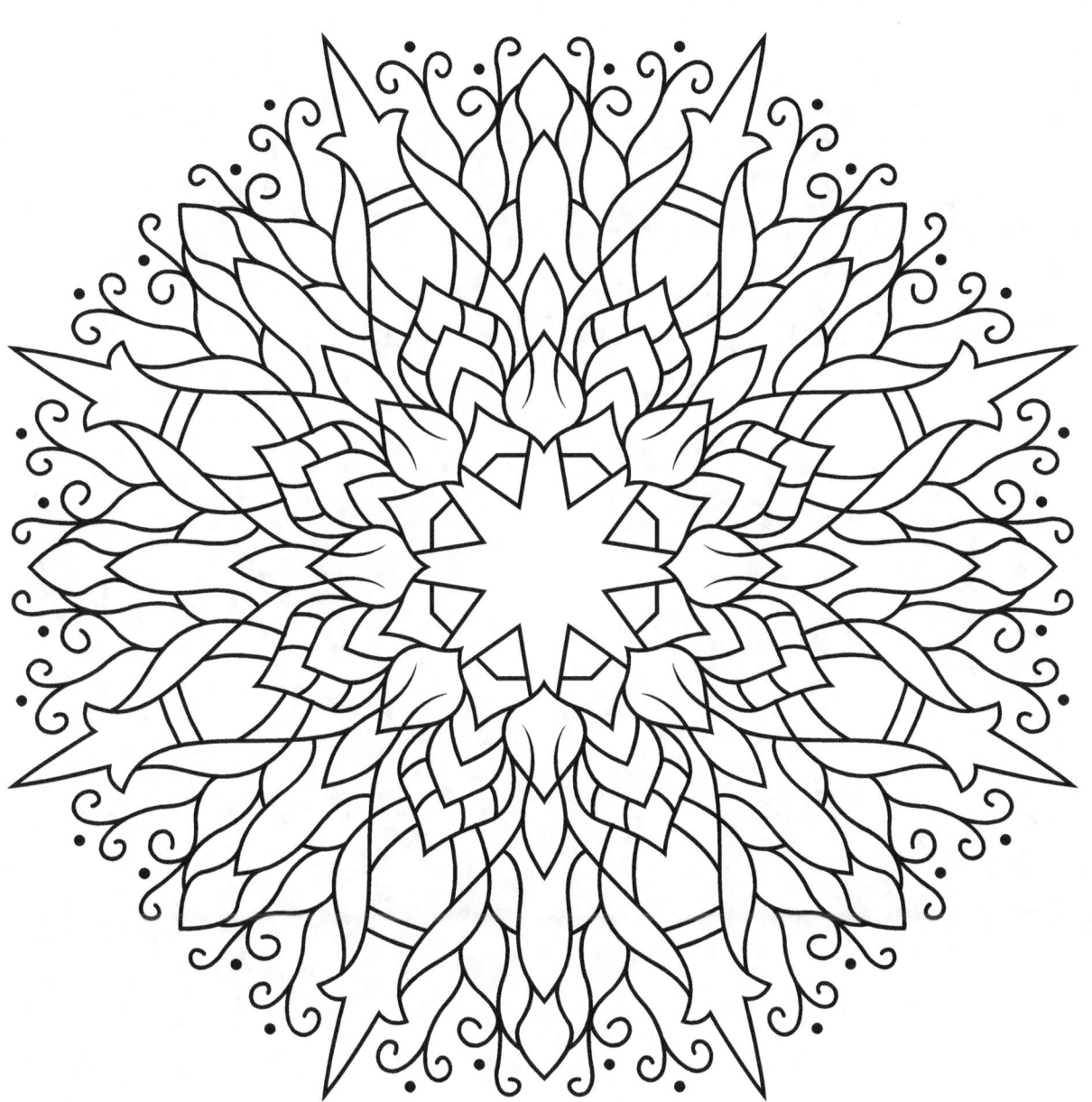

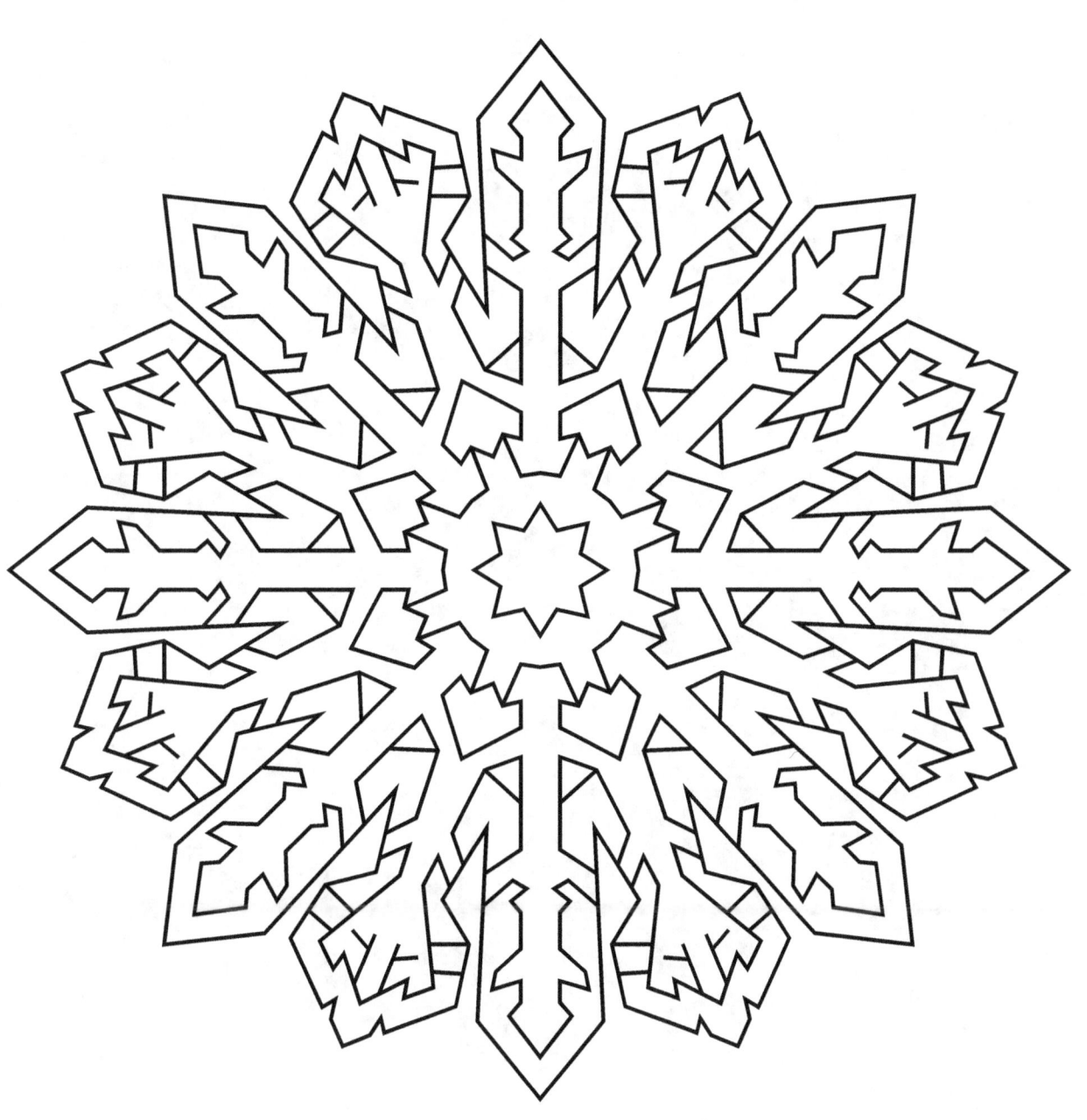

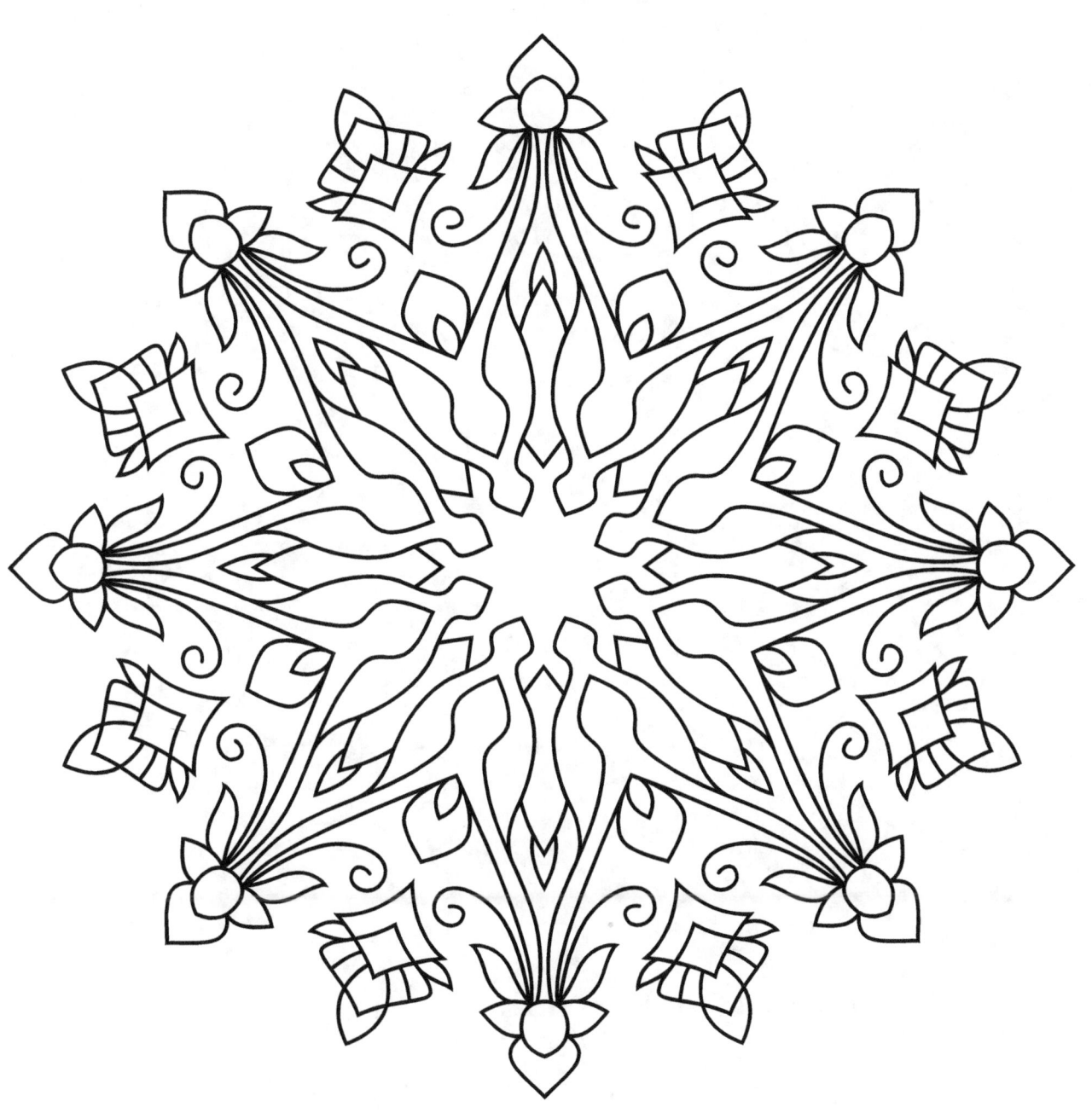

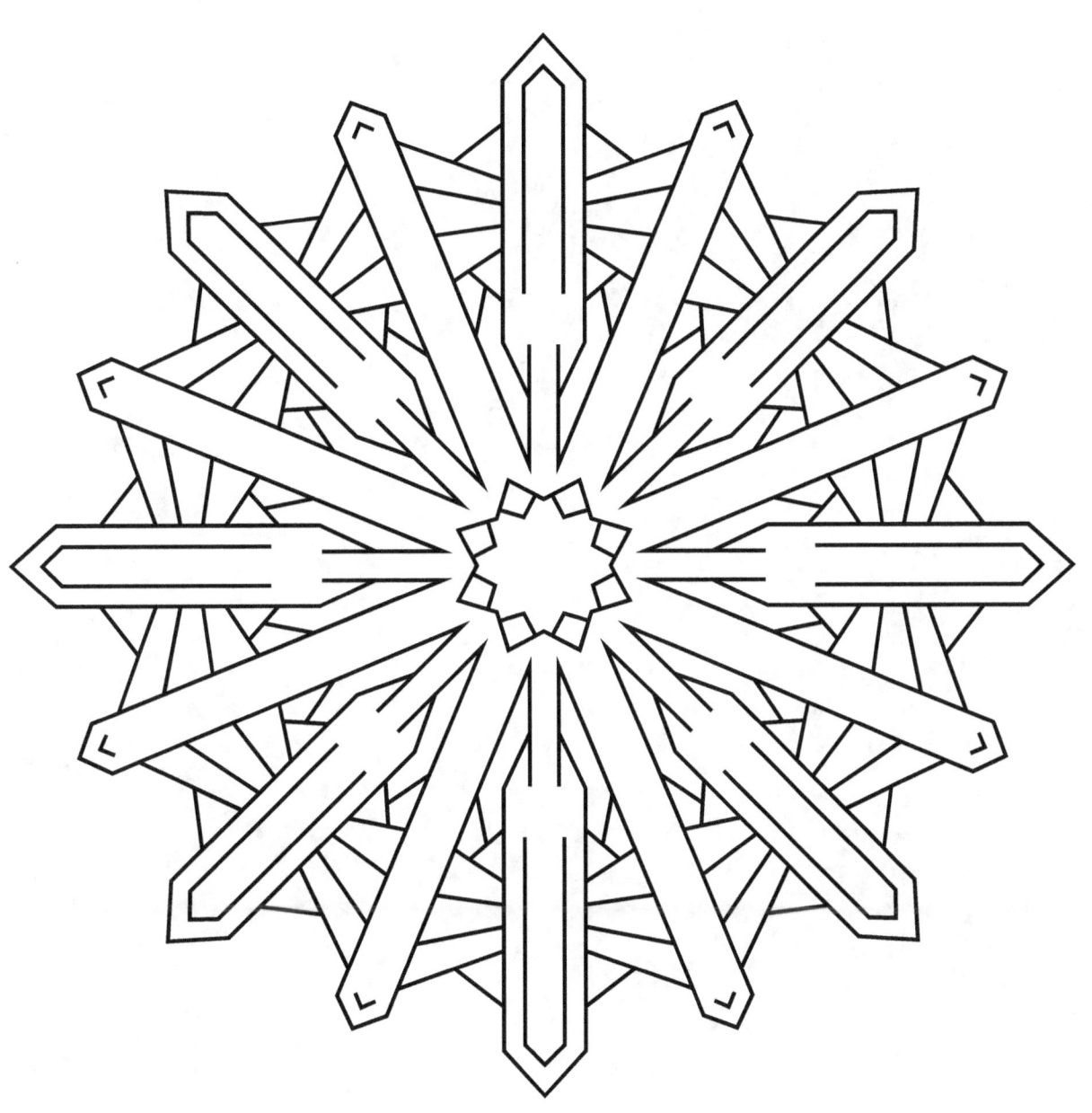

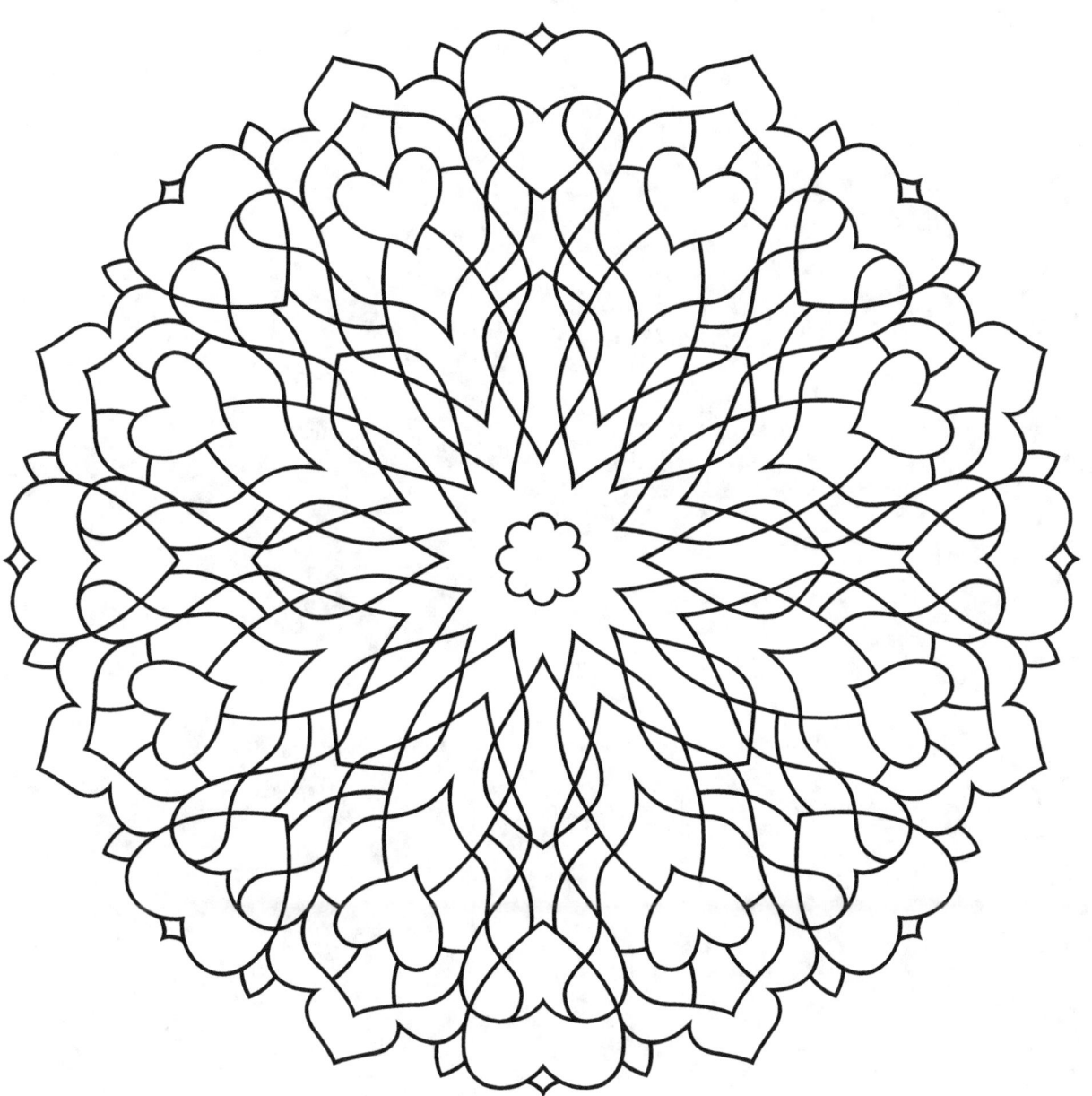

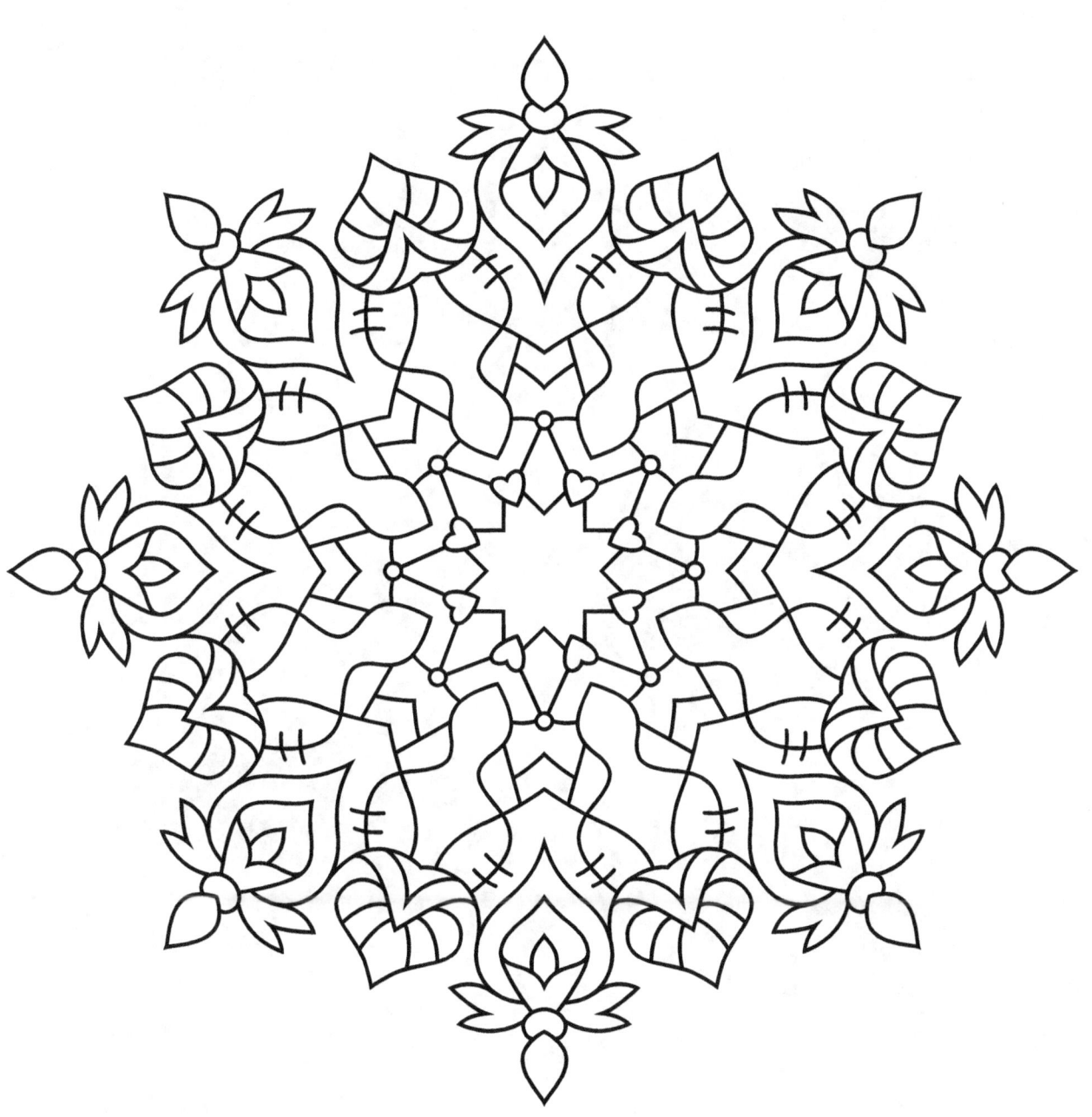

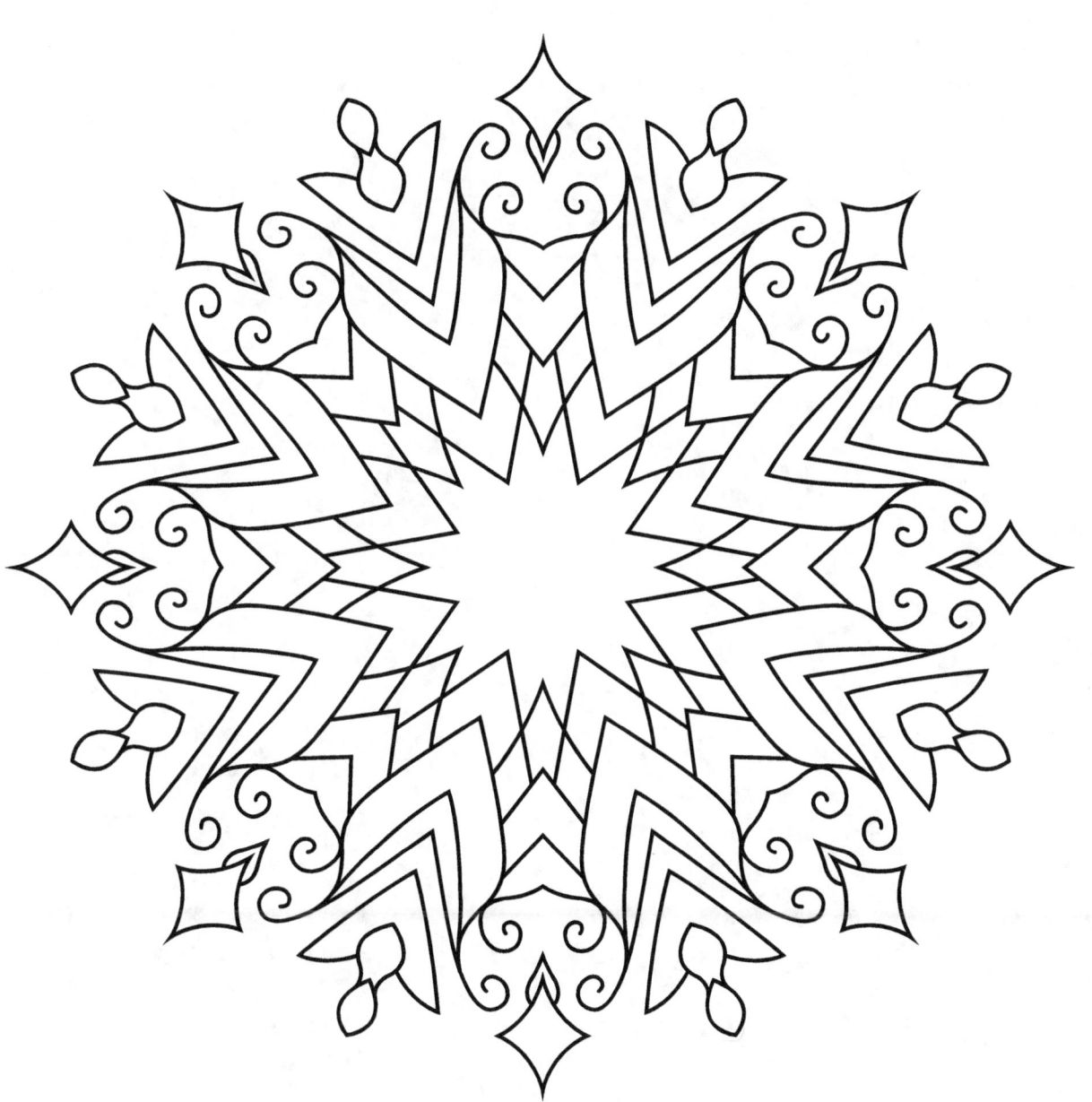

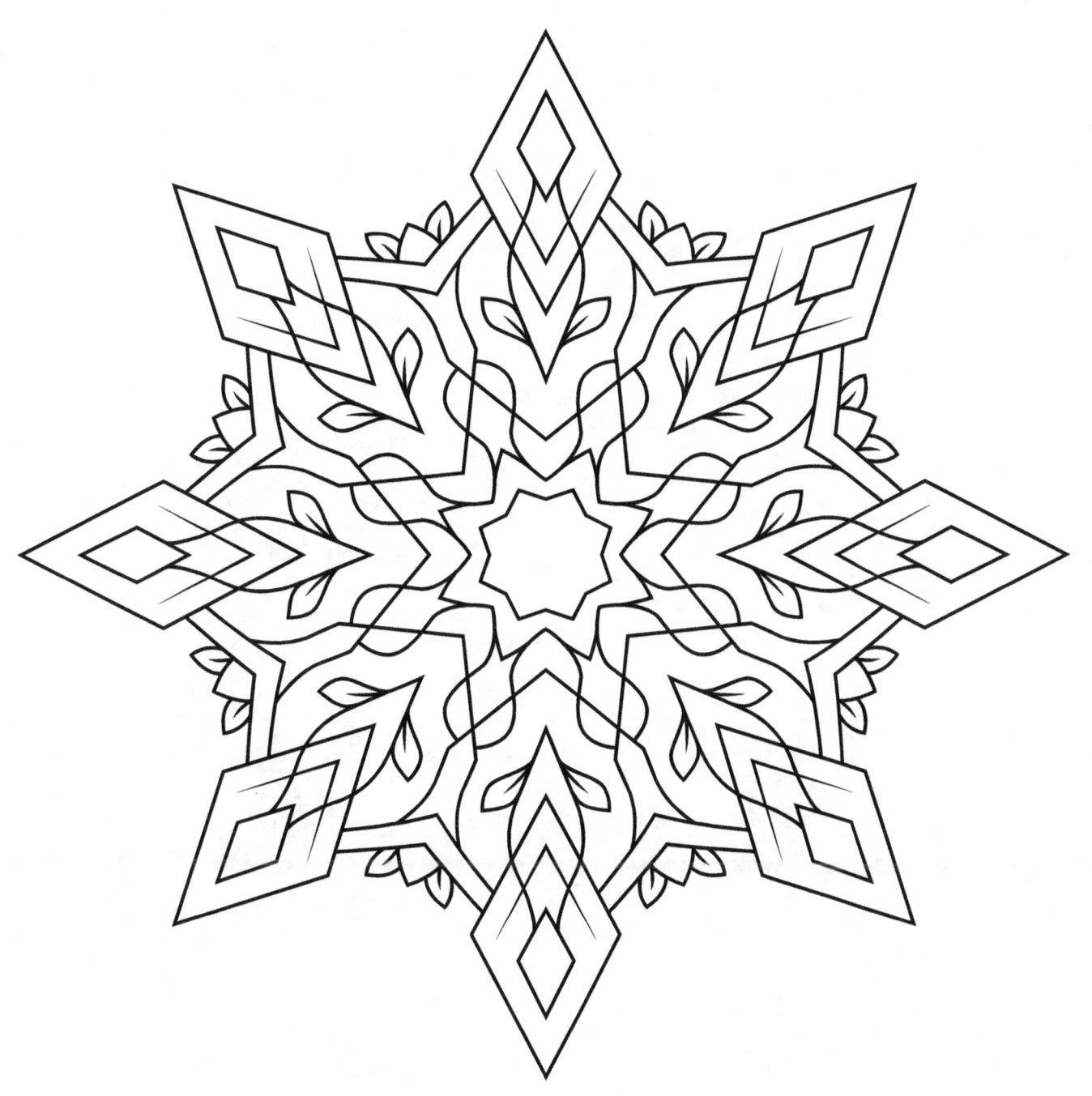

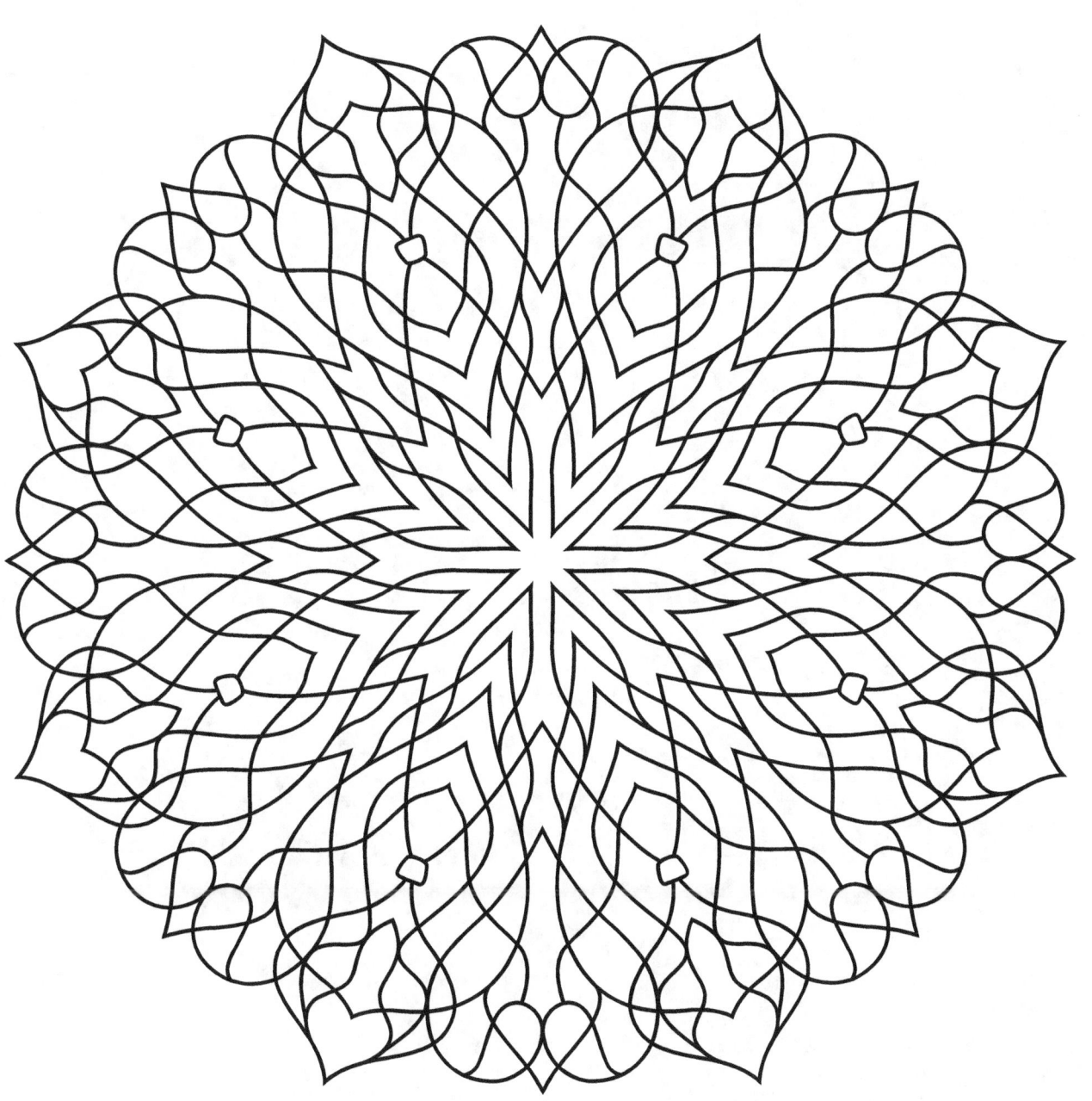

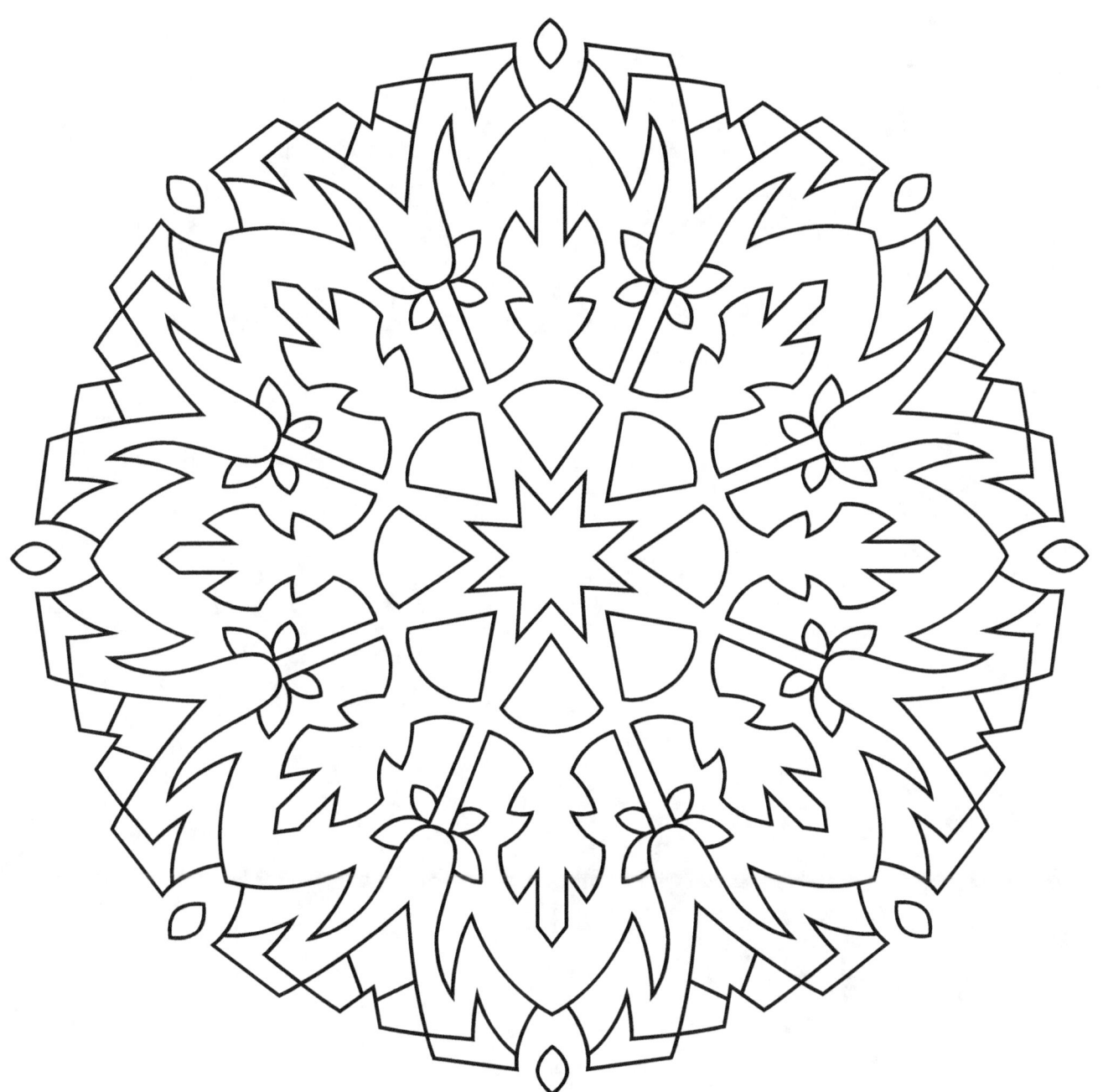

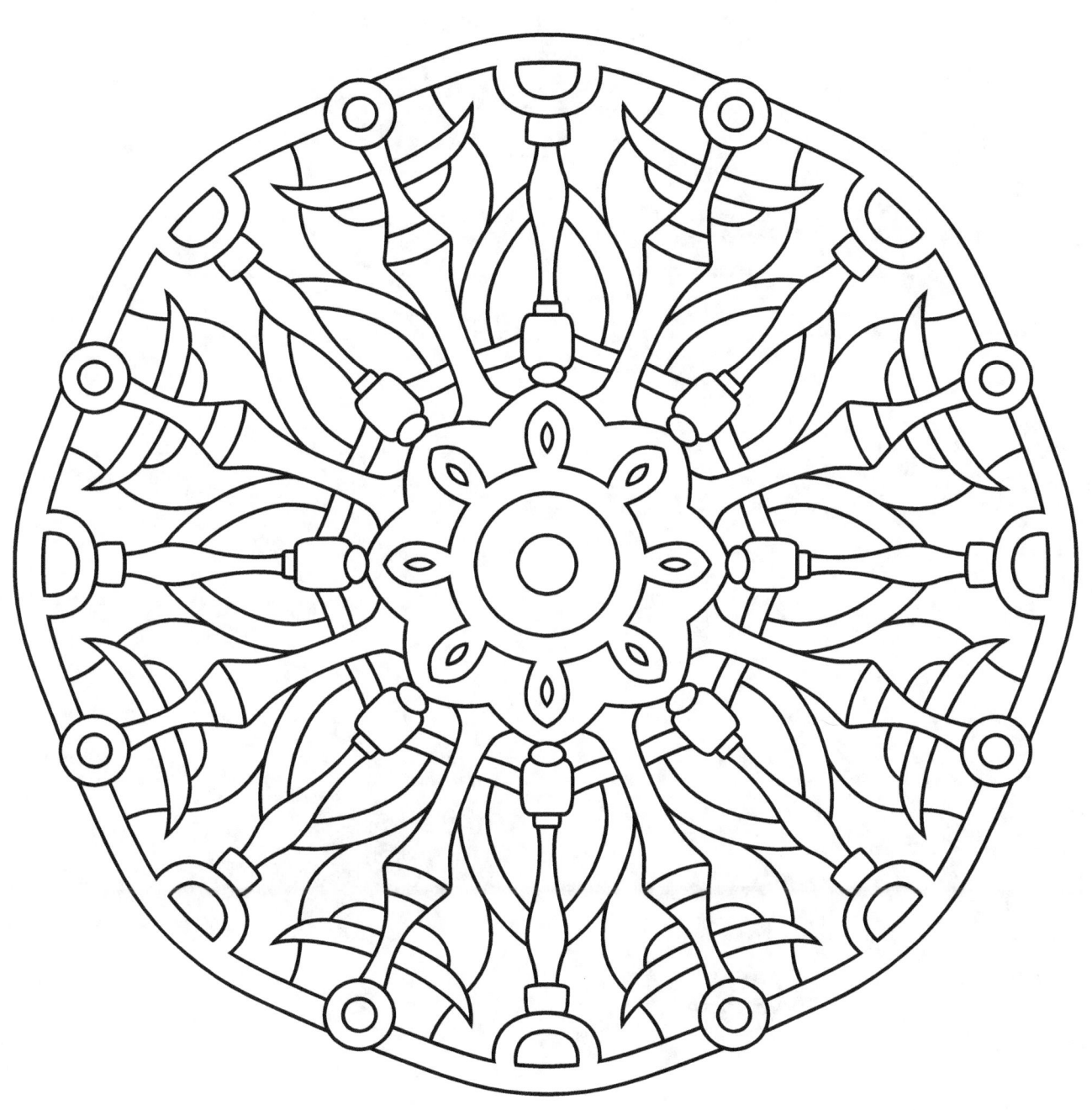

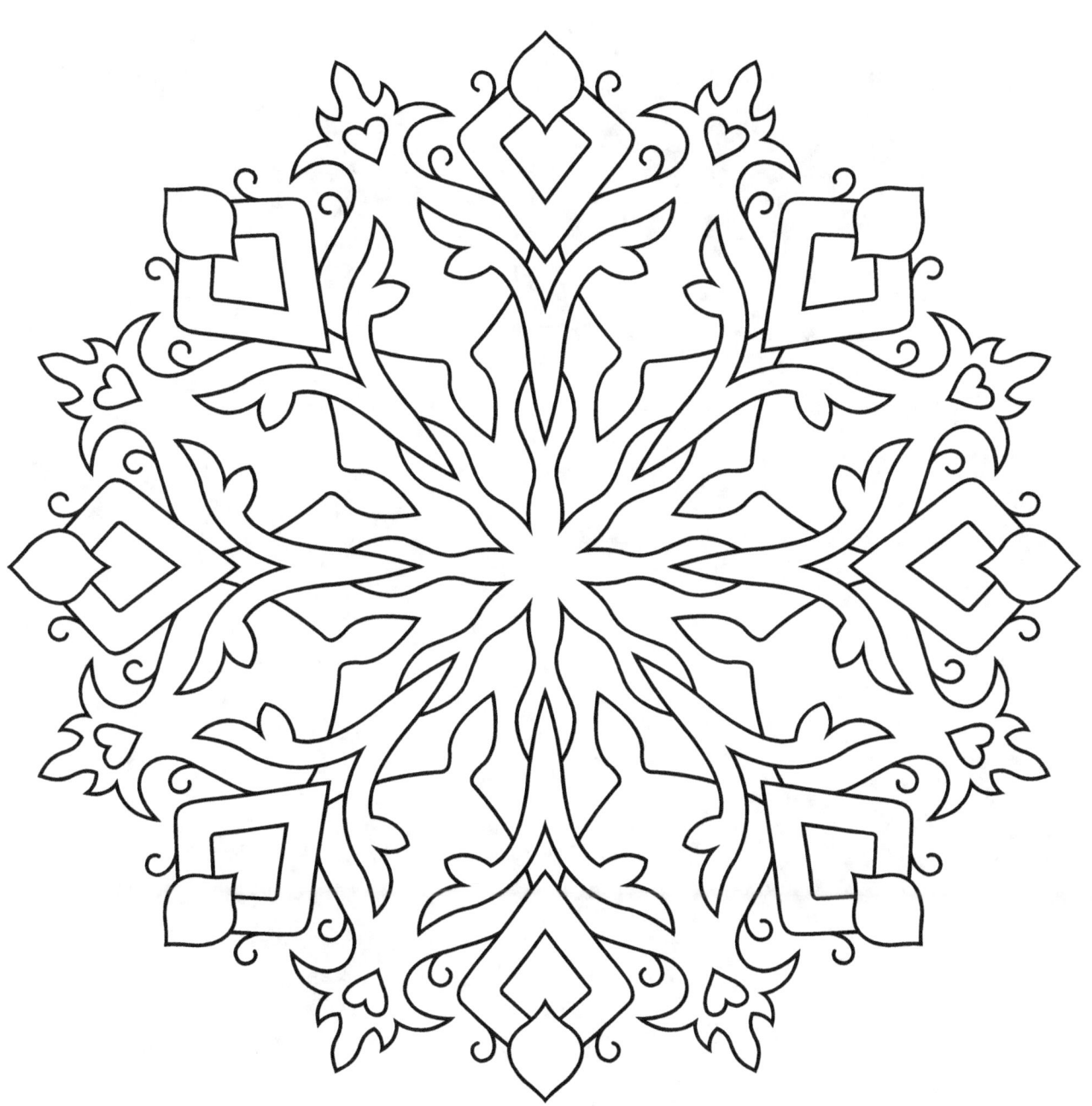

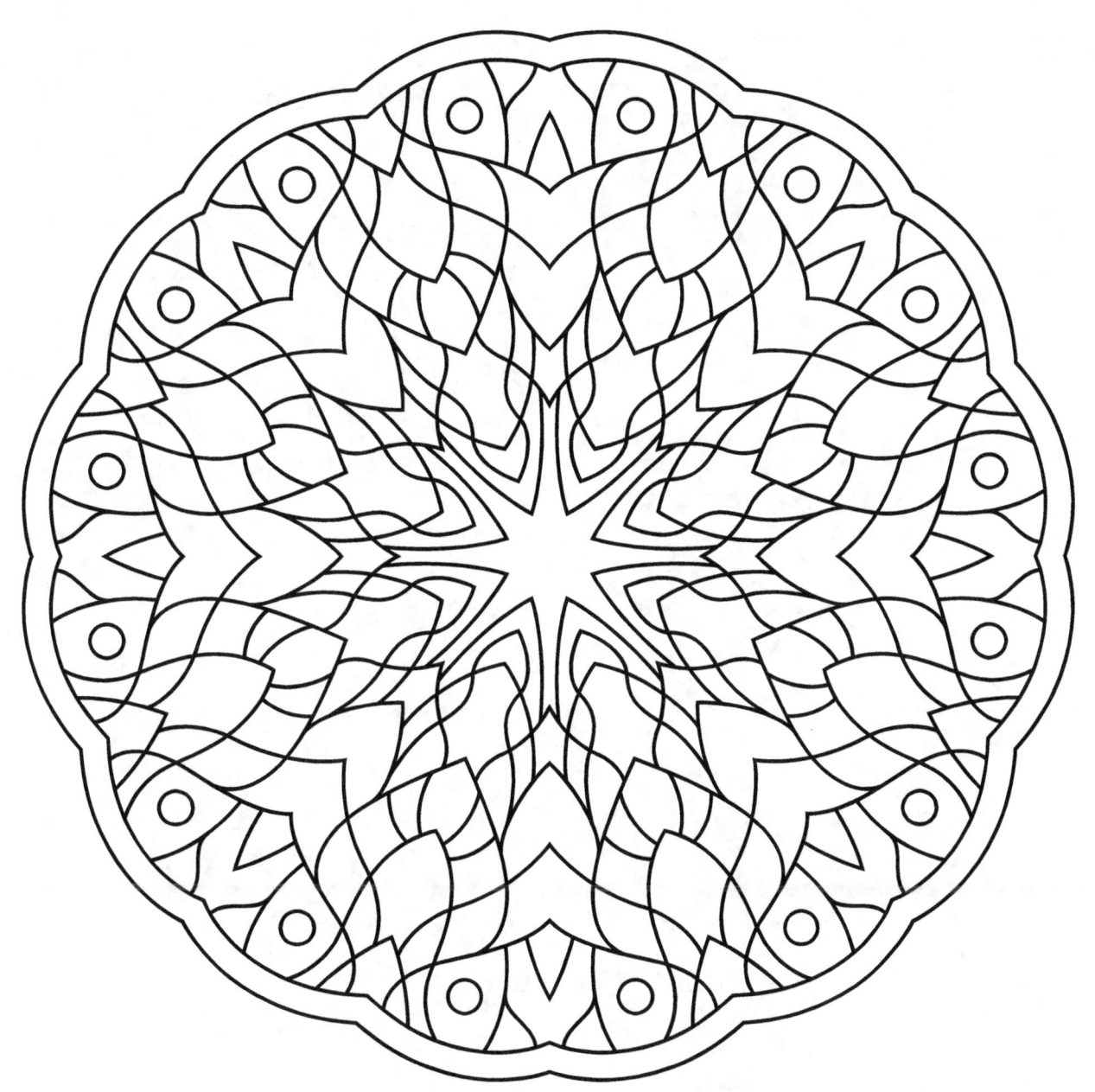

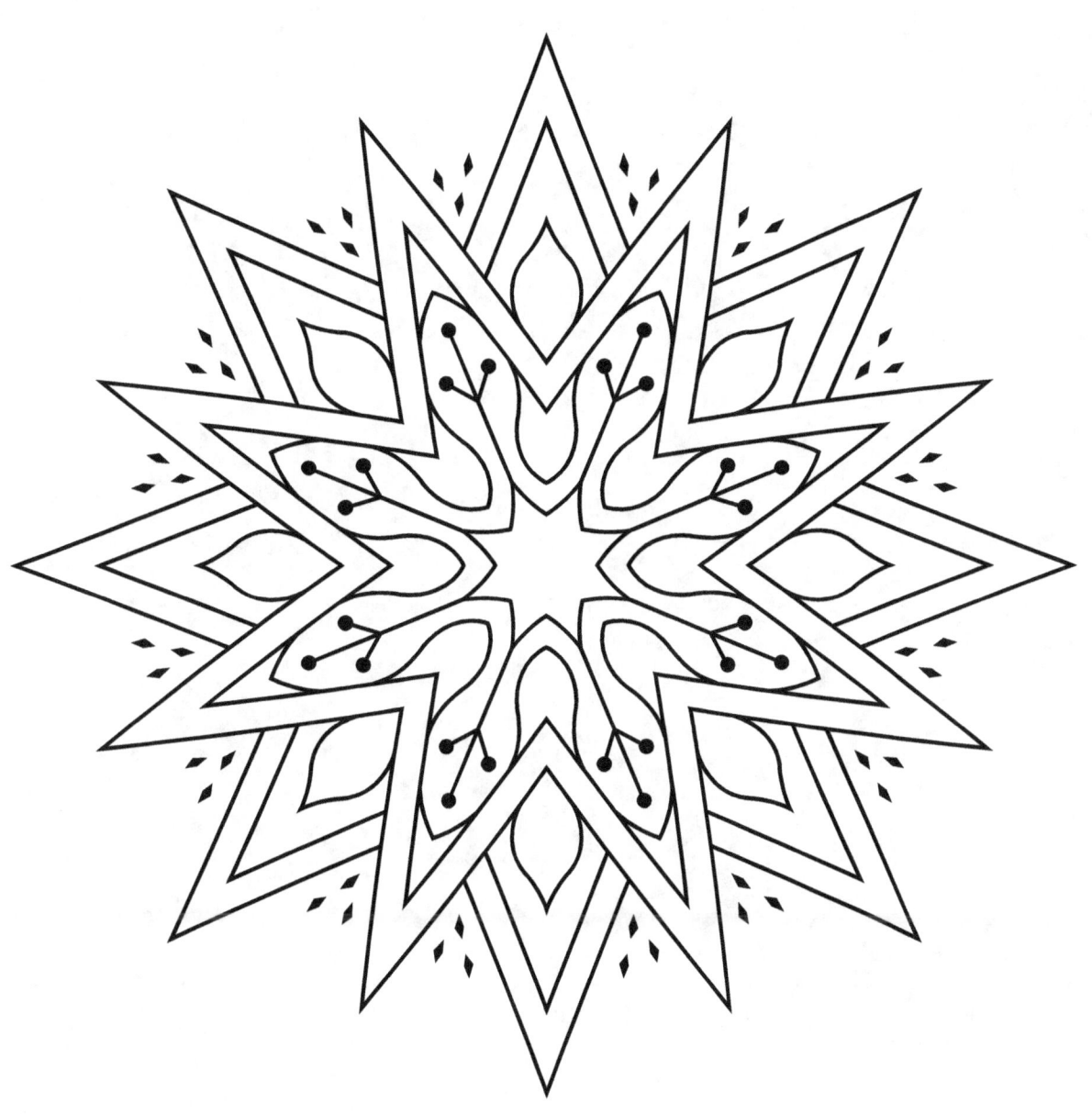

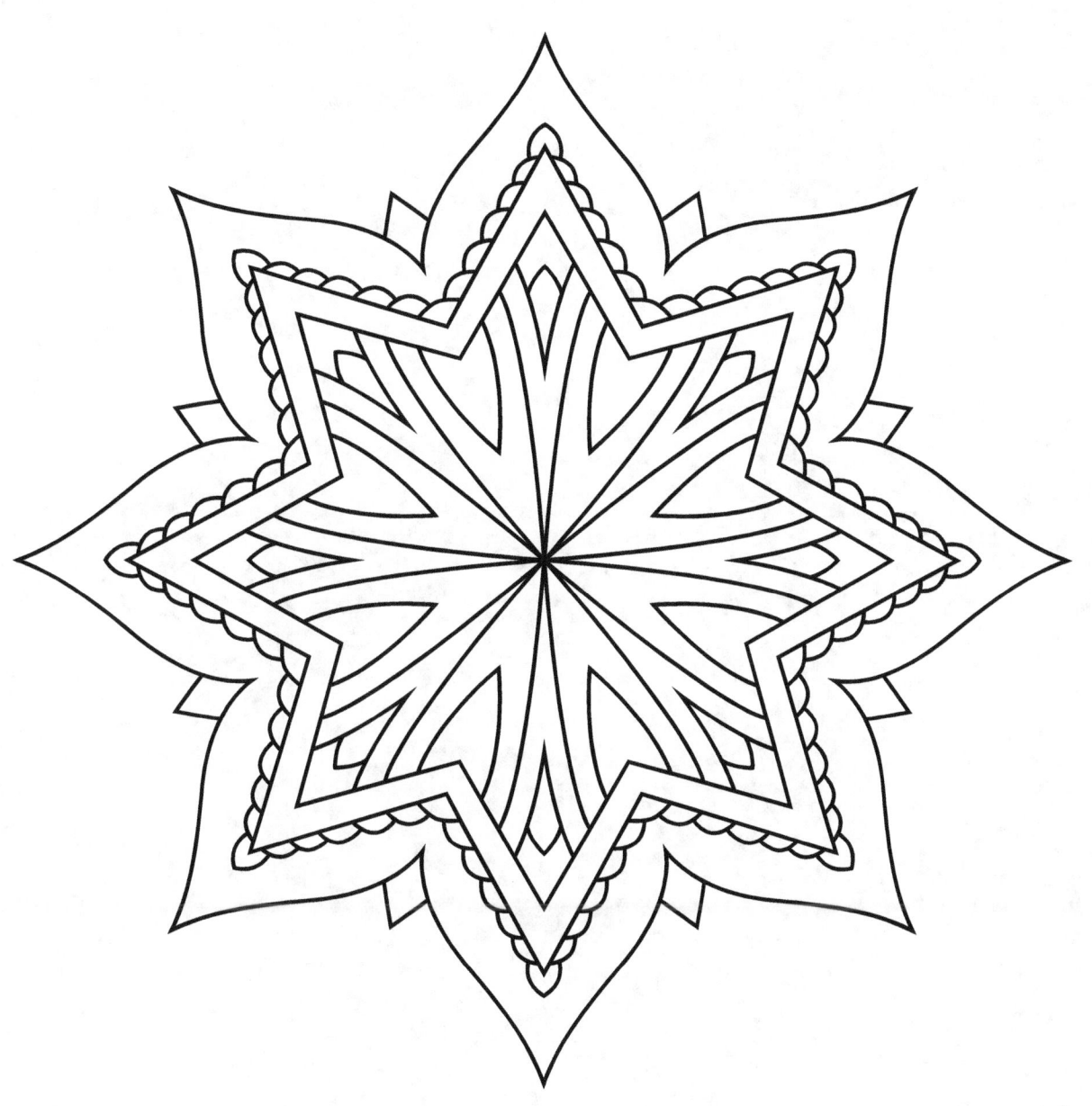

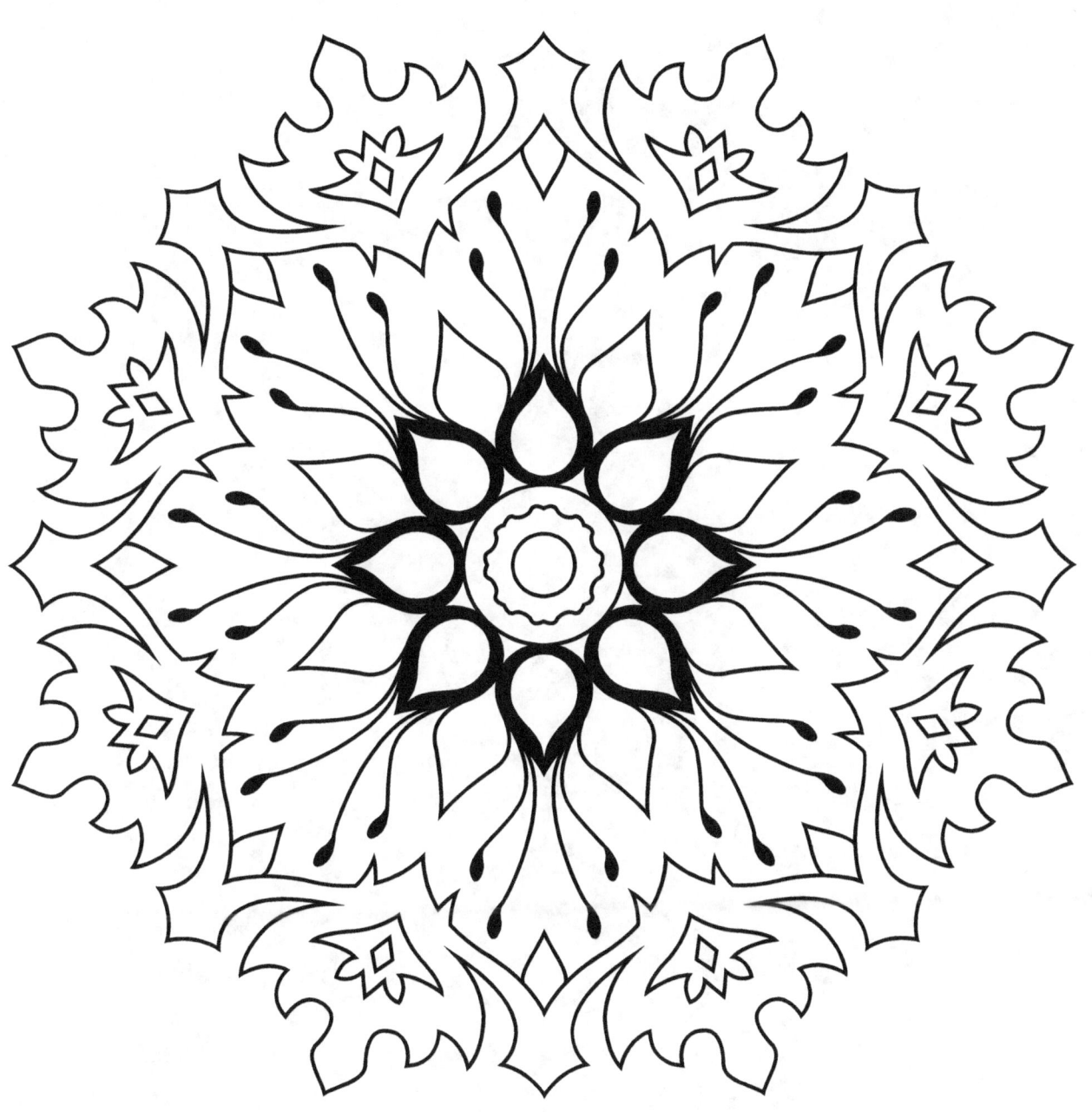

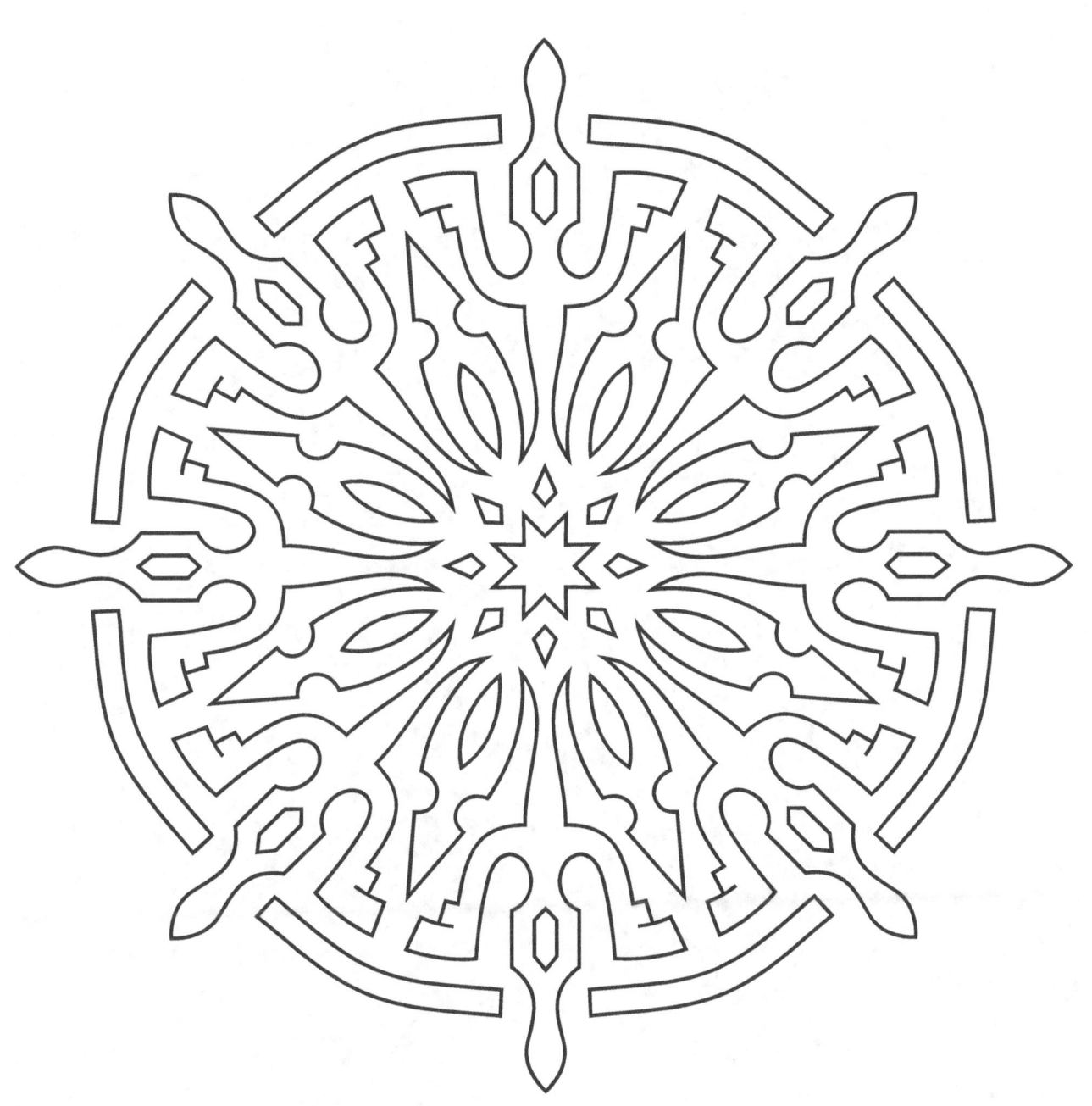

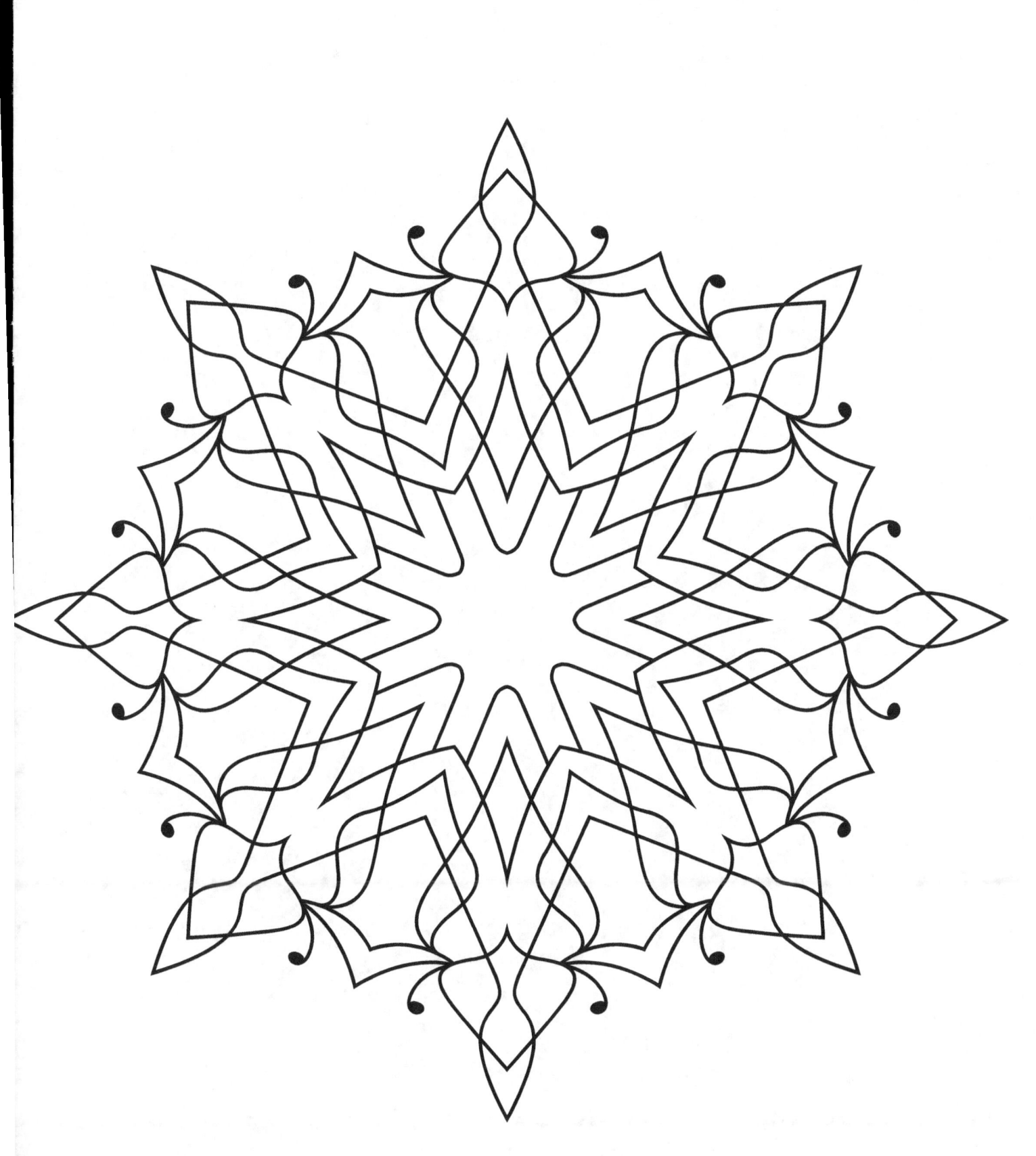

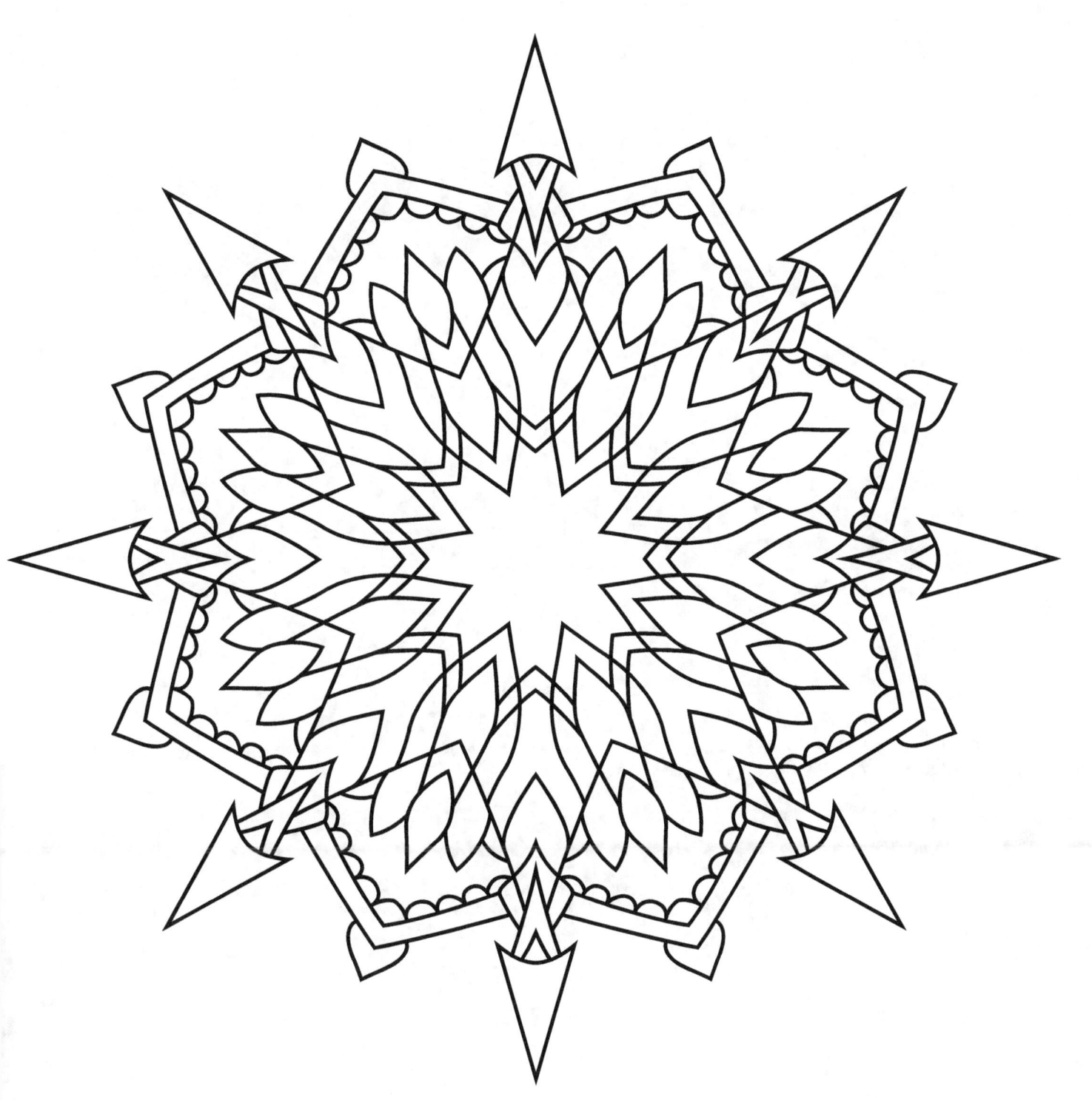

www.ingramcontent.com/pod-product-compliance
Lightning Source LLC
Chambersburg PA
CBHW080541220526
45466CB00010B/2997